SHADOW WORK
JOURNAL FOR
SELF-LOVE

Shadow Work Journal for Self-Love

Powerful Prompts and Exercises to Integrate Your Shadow and Embrace Your Inner Child

Valerie Inez & Latha Jay

ZEITGEIST • NEW YORK

All rights reserved.
Published in the United States by Zeitgeist, an imprint of Zeitgeist™,
a division of Penguin Random House LLC, New York.
zeitgeistpublishing.com

Zeitgeist™ is a trademark of Penguin Random House LLC
ISBN: 9780593690499
Ebook ISBN: 9780593690291

Book design by Aimee Fleck
Author photographs © by Jessica Danae Photography and Valerie Inez
Edited by Clara Song Lee

Printed in the United States of America
3rd Printing

*In loving memory of my father, Jay,
whose belief in the things I could do
was beyond my own vision.*

—Latha

*To my children. I chose to pursue
the path of healing to give you the
foundation you deserve.*

—Valerie

CONTENTS

BEFORE YOU BEGIN

Shadow work is the process of uncovering the parts of yourself that you try to hide, deny, or reject and bringing them into your awareness. It's finding the root causes of what's holding you back and processing them so that you can heal old wounds and break repetitive cycles that no longer serve you.

What to Expect from Shadow Work

Engaging in shadow work can be challenging, but the journey is deeply rewarding. Step by step, you discover and observe the parts of yourself you once kept hidden. Over time, you learn to accept these parts and better understand who you truly are. Inevitably, this process shines a light on the root causes of deep emotional pain, invites profound healing, and creates more room for self-love.

When we talk about self-love, we mean the deep appreciation of self that comes from accepting yourself fully, treating yourself kindly, and supporting your growth and well-being. Self-love is taking tangible actions that nurture your mind, body, and spirit.

How to Use This Journal

Begin by setting the intention to be gentle with yourself as you enter this uncharted territory. Shadow work can bring up triggers and intense emotions. It is vital that you work with compassion for your past and present self. If you struggle to deal with past memories, have a support system in place, such as a close friend, a mental health professional, or a spiritual advisor. There is no need to be alone on this journey.

This journal guides you through the work. Chapter 1 lays the foundation to prepare you for your journey. The wide range of exercises in Chapter 2 helps you identify your shadow parts, observe them with gentle awareness, and begin the journaling process. Chapter 3 guides you deeper, using journaling prompts to help you get to know more of your shadow self.

Here are a few suggestions to help you get the most out of this journal:

- Read Chapter 1 before trying any of the exercises and journaling prompts, and work through the Chapter 2 exercises before diving into Chapter 3.

- Follow your intuition. If an exercise doesn't resonate with you, skip it. If you want to jump around the journaling prompts in Chapter 3, that's okay. Use this journal in whatever way supports you best.

- Create space in your schedule to do shadow work *and* give yourself permission to deviate when you need to. Listen to your intuition and internal guidance. If something feels too uncomfortable, stop. Take a break and revisit it later. There is no due date for completing this work, and you will not be graded. Knowing this, you are free to just *be*, and to allow whatever comes up for you to truly come up.

- End each shadow work session with at least one self-care ritual that grounds and centers you. This will help integrate the healing that should take place after completing your shadow work sessions. We strongly believe that treating yourself with love, kindness, and compassion is a critical component of the shadow work journey, and self-care rituals comprise a big part of that.

Shadow work can be challenging, but it is worth it because you are worth it. Thank you for taking on this enormous task. You doing this work is a beautiful gift to *us*, the collective and the global community. We see you, we love you, and we appreciate you.

INTRODUCTION

We both came to shadow work during low points in our lives and have experienced firsthand how transformative this journey can be.

For me (Latha), shadow work started when I was hanging on by a thread to keep up appearances as a medical student. I woke up every morning feeling tired and deflated. I had spent so much time concerned about making others happy that I was miserable. Through shadow work, I began healing heartache from past relationships and breaking through self-imposed limits. I learned that my passion for helping people wasn't centered on the medical profession but rather on empowering people to better understand themselves.

For me (Valerie), shadow work began following my realization that I had difficulty managing my emotions; anger would often be my first reaction. I discovered that I was hiding a lot of sadness and felt uncomfortable in my own skin. When I started to do shadow work, I began to feel energetically lighter and got back in touch with my authentic self. It became easier to hear my own thoughts, and I found a connection to my intuition that I never had before.

Following our own experiences, we've guided hundreds of clients through this transformative process. Now we're excited to offer our support to you so that you can get back in touch with your inner light and truth, clear your energy, and remove limiting beliefs that prevent you from moving forward in your life. And remember, as we work on healing ourselves, we are actively working on healing the world.

1

The Shadow Work Journey

Shadow work has existed as long as humankind has been around, but it was popularized by psychoanalyst Carl Jung in the early 1900s. He wrote, "No tree, it is said, can grow to heaven unless its roots reach down to hell." To know the depth of our roots gives us the stability necessary to reach our highest achievements and truly know "heaven," our personal best life. This chapter lays the groundwork for you to look below the surface to discover the depth of your roots.

The Shadow and the Self

Understanding our shadows gives us a sense of control over them, and that gives us power. We no longer put energy toward suppressing them, which can be exhausting and damaging. Instead, we put our energy into getting to know ourselves and channeling that knowledge to various areas in our lives. This beneficial process is necessary for setting ourselves free. This exploration begins now.

Core Concepts and Ideas

The shadow self is made up of those parts of you that you subconsciously try to reject. It's in this space of rejection that your shadow self hides out. Your shadow self is comprised of those darker aspects (neither good nor bad) of your subconscious that remain hidden until you decide to consciously bring them to the forefront of your mind.

Your ego is the mask you wear that you consider your "identity" or your personality, which you use to thrive or survive in life. The tug of war you often feel within you is your ego challenging aspects of your shadow self, the repressed aspects of your identity.

Emotional wounds created during childhood can linger for a lifetime. It is in these moments of impactful events that we create an idea about ourselves. In the moment a child is ostracized by a classmate for fumbling during a speech, they might create and take on the idea that their voice doesn't matter, or isn't worthy of being heard. This idea can impact the rest of their life as they continue to reiterate it and believe it. It is in this repeated belief that a shadow is formed. This shadow will linger and show up in their adult life as never speaking up for themselves such as in moments of injustice, not asking for the job promotion, and not pursuing the partner they truly love. When we are able to do shadow work and heal these wounds, we are able to create a new, more empowering belief about ourselves and change our life.

People tend to repress their shadow parts because they have a strong emotional reaction to them. We rarely want to identify with the feelings of guilt, shame, or regret, and these feelings are the core of our shadow parts. Long-term repressed emotions can pop up in so many other ways. Years of carrying stress can show up as disease, anxiety, and other chronic issues. Thankfully, understanding these parts can release the negative emotions and make the shadow self less reactive, thereby relieving unnecessary stress.

How the Shadow Impacts Our Life

The shadow shows up in your life through triggers, projections, and patterns. Let's take a look.

A *trigger* is a reminder of a past trauma that causes a fight-or-flight response. Triggers occur as the result of deep, unresolved wounds that manifest through emotions like anger, fear, and anxiety, or the inability to express emotions. Think of these as messengers that allow us to be conscious and aware of what needs to be addressed within us. When you're immediately and consistently triggered by the same person or experience, ask yourself, "What needs to be addressed within me at this time?"

The world is a mirror. You create *projections* when you misinterpret what is coming from inside of you to be coming from outside of you. This is what's happening when you attribute traits or emotions you don't like about yourself to someone else.

Ever notice that it's the same stuff, but just on a different day? Same lousy boss at every job you work at? Different relationships ending the same way? These are *patterns*. We tend to create the same undesirable scenario repeatedly in our lives when we have not healed the pain behind it or when we have not looked closely enough to learn the lesson present in that scenario. Essentially, we begin running on autopilot when we allow our shadow selves to dictate our reality. This self-inflicted phenomenon is known among psychologists as "repetition compulsion."

Integrating our shadow happens one moment, one experience, one lesson at a time. It happens every time you have an opportunity to take a deep breath, pause, and reflect for a few seconds before responding to a situation. When we bring our shadow out into the light and accept it for who it is and how it contributes to our reality, our lives change for the better. This is called integration, and it happens when we truly accept and embrace all those parts of ourselves.

Shadow Work for Self-Love and Healing

Your shadow wants to be seen, heard, and accepted. Allow your shadow to emerge into the light and be healed. It is holding on to the wants and needs of your inner child, who desires to heal old childhood wounds; shadow work helps you love and heal your inner child. Connection between your shadow parts, inner child, and present human self helps you feel loved and accepted as a whole being.

We cannot "be the light" when holding another in the darkness, including ourselves. In other words, we can't be the light if we are holding aspects of ourselves in the darkness. However, the journey to self-love isn't always about "love and light." It's common to have ups and downs on this journey as you navigate your internal map. Some days may feel heavier than others, and that is completely valid. Surrender to the flow of these days and allow yourself to be fully present during this journey.

Shadow work offers you incredible healing, and through this healing comes strength. We feel better after we do this kind of work; we are better equipped and empowered to see our growth. Sometimes it's easier to think of healing a shadow in terms of a physical wound rather than an emotional one. You can only walk so far with a sprained ankle. When the ankle is healed, you can run.

Most importantly, healing looks different for everyone. There is no set timeline or hard-and-fast expectations to meet. However, healing—truly getting to a point of feeling better—takes self-dedication, time, and complete vulnerability with yourself. You are your own internal compass during this time and the only person who can measure your growth and healing.

How to Do Shadow Work

You can start doing shadow work anytime you feel ready or called to. Shadow work doesn't require any tools or materials to get started, but you can take several actions before you begin to make this journey more comfortable.

A Few Helpful Guidelines

Think of shadow work as a form of self-care. Set up the conditions to make this work comfortable and meaningful to you. Be sure to care for yourself before caring for others so you can show up to the outside world as the best version of yourself. Remember, this work primarily benefits you, but its wonderful results also benefit your loved ones.

Set aside time and space.

To begin, create a sacred routine that feels easy and natural. Set time aside in your day when you will be undisturbed to focus on shadow work. Grab a cozy blanket, light your favorite candle or incense, and find a comfortable spot. Dedicate this time for yourself to focus solely on this healing journey. We recommend an hour daily, but if you only get to fifteen minutes, that works too—make the most of what time you do have. Do what you can. There are no expectations other than those you place upon yourself. Be gentle and loving with yourself.

Trust in the power of mindful awareness.

When you begin to dive deeper within yourself, gradually developing an understanding of your shadow, you enter a state of mindful awareness. You become conscious of who you are and where aspects of your shadow have dominated your reality. With this awareness comes choice. You can choose to continue to allow your shadow self to remain unchecked in the darkness, or you can face it directly, send it love, and bring it to the light of your consciousness. Allow your shadow the space to exist within you, but also recognize that you are not the shadow. You are the awareness that *knows* when the shadow shows up in your experience.

Always practice self-compassion.

Self-compassion is just as crucial as awareness. When you treat yourself with compassion, you are able to get further in your shadow work journey. If you are having a hard time viewing your "bad" or "ugly" shadow parts without feeling shame, judgment, and/or guilt, remember that we all have these aspects. Your shadow is judged only by you. Release your self-judgment and replace it with love, forgiveness, and understanding.

Let yourself grow with courageous honesty.
Shadow work requires complete honesty with yourself, but that's not always easy. When you look at the work ahead of you, it might seem overwhelming and unapproachable. Please know that the fear of doing this work takes more energy than actually doing the work; fear is draining.

Once you step into shadow work, you will find your own flow that works for you, and the fear will disintegrate. It requires integrity to see yourself as a whole being and look at all parts.

You are not broken—nothing needs to be fixed. Shadow work allows you to live your life with more peace, freedom, and choice in all situations. This freedom comes with honesty, and the rewards are worth the temporary challenges.

When you are living in the self-created limits of your shadow, it crushes your ability to be truly who you are, in full self-expression, and you are constantly in a place of rejecting yourself. When you are repeatedly getting triggered, projecting your emotions, and repeating negative patterns, you are living a limited, exhausting life. Your journey's progress and success are worth the brief period of discomfort when facing yourself with complete honesty. On the other side is freedom.

Step-by-Step Shadow Work

Everyone's shadows are different, and everyone's journey to embracing themselves is unique. Shadow work activities and prompts may differ depending on where you look, but the general process of doing shadow work with this book may look something like this:

Ground and center yourself.

Grounding helps you be fully present within your body, connected to the security of the Earth and yourself. Grounding before engaging in shadow work can help you feel centered, balanced, and in a better state of mind. When you are grounded and centered, you are better able to respond to the world around you, rather than react to it. There are many ways to ground and center yourself to achieve a greater connection to self, such as meditation, spending time in nature, and doing yoga.

Journal with exercises and prompts.

Read the instructions and prompts, then take time to sit with them and let them sink in. You can choose to proceed with the prompts in the order they are currently structured or skip around, finding ones that appeal to you in any given moment.

There's no correct or wrong way to answer a question. What comes to you is what needs to flow in that moment. If you feel yourself getting stuck, try to write words that relate to a possible answer or even doodle for a moment. If you can't write sentences, write a list of words or phrases. Get as detailed as you wish, or keep your thoughts general if that feels more comfortable. You don't need to intellectualize what you are writing or try to label it.

Shadow work doesn't require you to intentionally revisit old memories or past traumas, but they may come up as you dive into a prompt. If you begin to feel overwhelmed by any memories that resurface, pause, take a deep breath, and ground and center yourself again. You are *here* now. If you feel overwhelmed or discouraged, give yourself space to feel and process these emotions. Seek support from a trusted friend, family member, or therapist.

It's important to allow yourself to feel and release any emotions that may come up. You are human, and feelings make up a significant part of our daily existence. However, if you do not have the capacity to continue a shadow work prompt because it feels too heavy, close your book and walk away. This is *your* journey! Maintain boundaries with yourself when you need to and also stay disciplined on other days when you feel able to do so.

Process and integrate.

It's important to check in with yourself and notice what's happening to process and integrate what's coming up. You must feel it to heal it. You can't go over it or under it—you have to go directly through the emotion and fully process it. When you go through an emotion, you are *growing* through it.

Keep in mind that there are no "good" or "bad" emotions. All emotions are completely valid, and learning to process them in a healthy way takes time. Allow yourself the space and time to deal with the emotions that arise and learn how to understand them. After years of suppressing some emotions, you may even find it difficult to feel any emotions at all.

Emotions are messengers offering us vital information on what action we need to take. Think of these as nuggets of inner wisdom that can offer you guidance along your journey. Be curious with yourself as these emotions surface. Remember, there is no judgment here. This is your journey to inner peace and freedom. Pay attention to your emotional reactions, as these will be telling. Shadow work is a lifetime process. As we live, shadows are created, but with knowledge of this, we can process and integrate them as we go.

Conclude with self-compassion.

Self-compassion is vital to shadow work. While love and kindness should be present throughout the shadow work process, including an intentional moment of self-compassion as you finish the day's work can help you feel settled, complete, and clearer about what came up. However, even with the presence of love and kindness, you may leave a shadow work session feeling a bit angry, disappointed, or upset. It happens! We've been there. Spend some time resettling yourself by taking a few deep breaths, ground yourself as needed, and allow yourself to process any emotions you need to. Be compassionate with yourself for however you feel.

Supportive Self-Care Rituals

Supportive self-care rituals can help keep you engaged with your shadow work and connected to why you are cultivating more love for yourself, including your shadow parts. Self-care involves taking care of your mind, body, and spirit, because you are so deserving of it.

Connecting back to yourself through any of the following rituals allows you to reconnect with your heart and the entire reason you are embarking on this journey. We highly recommend using any of these self-care rituals to ease some of the pain that may arise when uncovering your hidden truths and, in general, as you are finishing up a shadow work session.

Meditate to ground and center. Meditation can also help you process and release energy when you're feeling intense emotions or help you discern the cause of a trigger.

Connect with nature by stepping outside. Allow the sun to shine on your face. Listen to the world around you. Smell the scent of the earth. Gaze at plant or animal life.

Ground your energy by putting your bare feet on the earth or lying on the ground. This helps your body electrically reconnect you to nature and essentially resets your system.

Spend time with your animal companion(s). Interacting with your pets, if you have them, can ease anxiety and stress and encourage playfulness.

Enjoy life beyond the screen. Your phone is helpful in so many ways, but it can be a huge drain on your energy. Don't go straight to your phone following shadow work, and set up regular times to put your phone away for a bit to simply enjoy life.

Immerse yourself in music. Listen to your favorite playlist, dance, and sing. Singing is a phenomenal way to connect with your voice.

Eat something delicious. Food provides comfort, warmth, and love. Show yourself this kindness and enjoy something you love to eat. Take time to savor it, and express gratitude to the food for nourishing your body.

Play and have fun. Do something that makes you laugh or brings you joy. Remember what it feels like to be a kid again, fully present and immersed in moments that bring laughter and silliness.

Commit to setting healthy boundaries. Sometimes shadow work reveals the need for stronger boundaries. In such cases, make a commitment to set one or more. Visualize yourself setting the boundary or practice what you'll say to set the boundary.

Move your body in any way that feels good to you. Lift weights, go for a run, shake it out, or dance to your favorite music. Your body is an amazing machine that needs movement to release stagnant energy. Get your heart beating and blood flowing.

Take a nap or go to bed early. Sleep is vital to your emotional stability and joy. It's common to put it in last place because everything else seems more important. But to recharge, you need to sleep, so give yourself permission to turn in early or take a nap.

Schedule ME time into your weekly schedule. Take some time to prioritize yourself and plan to do something you really love to do, and commit to it.

Do some yoga. Yoga is a great practice to remind you that you are in competition only with yourself. It helps reconnect your mind and body by grounding and centering you.

Journal without your inner critic looking over your shoulder. Whatever you write is right. Let the words flow on the page. The practice called "Morning Pages" in which you free write, created by Julia Cameron, encourages you to let words pour out of you each morning as soon as you wake up; you can also do this following a shadow work session.

Practice gratitude. Notice good things and appreciate them. Express gratitude to yourself. List five to ten things you are grateful for.

Organize something. Whether it's organizing your mail or beauty supplies, bringing order to something that is in disarray can help bring a sense of inner calm or relaxation.

Clean and cleanse your space. We are energetic beings interacting with other energetic beings, and this is no more obvious than when we are doing shadow work. Cleanse your space in whatever manner feels comfortable to you to leave it feeling peaceful and harmonious.

Take a relaxing bath. Sitting in a warm bath can be so grounding and comforting. Light a candle, fill the bath with bubbles, and sprinkle in some rose petals or whatever feels nourishing.

Learn something new. Read a few pages of a book that interests you, research a topic you are curious about, or listen to an interesting podcast.

Drink water. Staying hydrated lets your body function as it's meant to. Drinking water throughout your day helps everything move easier. After shadow work, it's an excellent way to feel refreshed.

Watch your favorite movie. Put on a movie that makes you laugh or gives you a sense of childhood nostalgia. Make a healthy snack and relax.

Change into something nice. Whatever dressing up means to you, do it. When we look polished on the outside, we shift our internal energy just a bit.

Connect with others. Reach out to someone who loves you, someone who celebrates you rather than just tolerates you, and has the type of energy you want to be around.

State affirmations. Daily affirmations can shift your mindset by slowly reprogramming your subconscious. Have a few in mind to use following your shadow work session and throughout the day.

2

Exercises and Activities

The exercises and activities in this chapter help you access, process, and integrate your shadow self. Feel free to start with exercises and activities that feel most accessible to you, skip exercises that don't resonate, and repeat exercises you find particularly helpful as often as you'd like.

Mirror Work

Mirror work, a powerful practice in which you gaze at yourself in a mirror, is literally an in-your-face way to face your shadow. Limiting beliefs, fears, and doubts may surface, and aspects of your shadow may appear and repulse you. Be sure to treat yourself with compassion throughout this practice and after.

1. Sit or stand comfortably in close range to a mirror.
2. Look into your eyes for two to three minutes, and as you do so, repeat a compassionate affirmation in your mind or aloud. Motivational author Louise Hay encouraged saying "I love you" during mirror work. If that's too difficult, try "May I be able to love myself sometime in the future." Use whatever positive affirmation works best for you.
3. As you repeat the affirmation, notice what thoughts and emotions come up for you. Allow yourself to feel whatever comes up in that moment, and be present with it.

JOURNAL PROMPT: What thoughts came up? What emotions came up? How do you feel now? What, if anything, did you discover about yourself during this mirror work session?

Challenge Limiting Beliefs

Challenging your limiting beliefs, which are shadow aspects of yourself, is a powerful exercise to train your mind to choose a different path. Doing this consistently can significantly shift the way you think by helping your brain create new neural pathways, which supports your overall well-being and growth.

1. Draw three columns on a piece of paper. Title the columns "Limiting Belief," "How It Affects Me," and "Challenging Thought."

2. In the first column, list your limiting beliefs. Two examples are "Nobody could ever love me" and "I'm not good at anything."

3. In the second column, state how each belief affects you. For example, "Because I feel unlovable, it's hard to connect with people" and "I don't try new things because I think I will fail."

4. In the third column, challenge those beliefs. One way is to write the opposite of your limiting belief. For example, "I *am* lovable. When I show up as my authentic self, I attract people who love me" and "I *am* good at some things, and I can try something new without worrying if I will be good at it or not."

JOURNAL PROMPT: When you think of a limiting belief, where do you feel it in your body? Why do you think you feel it there? What emotions are associated with that limiting belief? How is the limiting belief connected to those emotions?

Write a Letter to Your Younger Self

Younger versions of ourselves often still live in fear and need to be seen, heard, validated, loved, and nurtured. You can connect with your inner child and bring healing to an issue through letter writing.

1. Think about yourself as a child. Identify a moment when you could have used some advice or help.

2. Begin your letter with "Dear Younger Self" or address a certain age or time period in your life—for example, "Dear Seven-Year-Old Me."

3. With complete vulnerability and honesty, write to that younger version of yourself. Offer the advice you needed to hear at that time. Share whatever thoughts your younger version could have benefitted from.

4. Describe how hearing this advice during that important time in your life would have changed things for you.

5. Express empathy for your younger version and close out your letter with love.

JOURNAL PROMPT: In what ways, if any, do you allow your inner child to freely express themselves as a loved and nurtured part of your being? Do you keep your inner child locked away in the shadow? If so, why? What might happen if your inner child was permitted full expression?

Dreamwork

Dreamwork, the process of writing your dreams down and exploring their meaning, helps you investigate the hidden shadow aspects of yourself. The more you do this, the easier it becomes to remember your dreams and learn from them.

1. Keep a journal by your bed. Set an intention to remember your dreams.
2. When you wake up, write down anything you remember.
3. In your journal, explore the following questions:

   - What recurring people, places, or events appear in your dreams? What emotions do they bring up? What might they symbolize?
   - Do your dreams offer a metaphorical solution to a problem or situation in your life? (Dream interpretation websites and books can help you here.)
   - What do the characters in your dreams represent? Which of their characteristics are important to you?

JOURNAL PROMPT: Describe a disturbing dream or nightmare. If the discomfort or fear in this dream or nightmare were real, what would you have to do to face it and move beyond it?

Fill in the Blanks

This exercise helps you explore what's been hidden so that you may live in more alignment with your true self.

1. Fill in the blanks with the *first* thought, word, emotion, or image that comes to your mind. There are no right or wrong answers.
2. At the end, read the entire paragraph back to yourself and notice what emotion(s) this elicits.

When I get upset or frustrated, I run to _____ to cope with how I'm feeling. If that is not readily available, I feel _____. I've been in this pattern of behavior for _____ years. When I was younger, I saw my caregivers _____ when they were feeling upset or frustrated. _____ brings me a sense of calm. I am tired of feeling _____ and _____. Instead, I want to try _____ to help myself when I'm feeling this way. Growing up, I was told _____. Hearing that for so many years has made me feel _____. This has impacted my life by _____. I am scared of _____. I know that I am worthy of _____ and _____. I deserve _____.

JOURNAL PROMPT: What patterns of behavior did you learn from your caregivers, family, friends, and/or society that don't add value to your life? How are you repeating those negative cycles?

Reflective Writing

This exercise allows you to sit back and reflect on certain aspects of your life in order to bring unseen emotions to the surface to be examined. By taking this moment to pause, untangle the sea of thoughts, and create a new meaning behind them, you can redirect your energy to take new action steps aligned with your future.

1. Ask yourself each of the following questions. Go in order, writing down your responses to each question in your journal.

   - What am I feeling right now?
   - What else am I feeling?
   - What in my life is causing me to feel this way?
   - How are these feelings currently impacting my life?
   - Do I wish to continue to feel this way? If not, what can I do to transmute these feelings and move through them?
   - Next time I feel this way, what is one thing I can do to improve my state of mind?

JOURNAL PROMPT: When you are feeling uninspired, confused, or lost, describe how you treat yourself. Are you kind or punishing? In what ways do you freely express yourself?

Be Creative

Children are natural creators, but, as adults, many of us push this creative nature aside for actions that produce something with outside value. In this exercise, you do not need to produce anything for anyone but you. Let your inner child be fully self-expressed. There are no rules or restrictions. You can even get messy. If you find this activity to be therapeutic, schedule time to do it regularly.

1. Set aside a minimum of 30 minutes to create something.
2. Think about the specific ways you liked to create and what brought you joy as a child.
3. Choose a creative medium such as clay, paint, markers, or pencils, and get your materials together.
4. Now, simply create whatever comes to you.

JOURNAL PROMPT: When you were a child, what did you most want to be when you grew up? How did dreaming of doing this make you feel? Why did this dream bring you joy? Consider the ways in which you create joy in your life. If you don't make time for joy in your day, what's stopping you?

Meditate

Meditation complements shadow work because it helps you create stability within yourself in the midst of outer and inner upheaval. While there is no goal in meditation, it assists you in responding to the world rather than being triggered by it. We don't meditate to get good at meditation; we meditate to get good at life. Meditation can be as simple as breathing; this particular one includes the use of a phrase or mantra for focus.

1. Find a quiet place to sit on a chair or the floor. Sit with your spine extended and with your head up as if you are balancing a crown. It is best to sit on a firm surface rather than on your bed or couch, where you're more likely to fall asleep.

2. Pick a short phrase or mantra that resonates with you and brings you peace. A great mantra to use is "so hum," which means "I am." It reminds us that we are so much more than just our shadows.

3. Set a timer for 10 to 20 minutes and close your eyes. The Insight Timer app is great for this.

4. Breathe normally and repeat your phrase or mantra in your mind's voice. As thoughts come to you, notice them without responding; bring your attention back to your phrase or mantra as often as necessary until the timer chimes.

JOURNAL PROMPT: What phrase or mantra did you select? Why does it bring you peace? During your meditation session, what thoughts or feelings came up? What shadows are you currently addressing?

Write a Letter to Your Future Self

Addressing your future self allows you to send love, gratitude, and acceptance to that version of you, regardless of what you might achieve or accomplish. Use this as a moment to practice self-love now and in the future.

1. Begin your letter with "Dear Future Self" or address a certain age or period in your life.

2. Describe what's going on presently. What are you grateful for? What are your insecurities and worries? Be honest and descriptive.

3. Describe your current and future goals. Don't be hardwired to one specific path; instead, give gratitude to your future self for all they've accomplished. There are infinite possibilities your future version can take based on the actions you choose today.

4. Describe where you see your future self. In what ways are you different? What is your proudest accomplishment? Be mindful of any self-doubt, feelings of unworthiness, fear, anxiety, or pessimism that come up. Keep expressing love and gratitude for future you.

5. Read your letter aloud. How will your future self feel reading this?

6. Put your letter someplace safe. Set a reminder to read it, perhaps a year or more from now.

JOURNAL PROMPT: What resistance or doubt came up when writing and/or reading the letter? What steps can you take to align yourself with a more confident and empowered version of you?

Converse with Your Shadow

Your voice is your connection to the outside world. When you allow yourself to speak freely, you give yourself the freedom of uninhibited expression. Have you ever said or done something that felt out of character? That was a shadow part of you! This exercise allows you to connect with and understand those shadow aspects of yourself by having an inner conversation with your shadow.

1. Keep an open mind, and think of some questions you would like to ask your shadow. For example, think of a time when you reacted in a way that felt out of character for you. What aspects of your personality feel like they are difficult to maintain? You can ask your shadow any question you are curious about.

2. Now wait for an answer from your shadow. What comes to mind after you ask your question?

3. Keep the dialogue going between you and your shadow as long as you need to in order to obtain a clear answer.

4. Document the answers in a journal or voice recording. After bringing these aspects of yourself to the light of your consciousness, you can befriend and integrate these parts of you, instead of making them your enemy. Awareness is key!

JOURNAL PROMPT: What part of your personality are you hiding from the world? Do you show up as your authentic self or do you put on a mask around certain people or environments? Why do you do this?

Mirror High Five

Author Mel Robbins came up with the "High 5 Habit" when she was at her lowest. It's about taking a moment to appreciate ourselves instead of immediately pointing out what's wrong with us or what we want to be different (for example, having too many wrinkles, not being thin enough, or having too many blemishes). When you step into your day by giving yourself a high five, it shuts up that judgmental voice for a moment and gives you space to direct your mind elsewhere. This might sound silly, but try it every day for two weeks and see how you feel.

1. When you wake up in the morning and start your day, look at yourself in the mirror.
2. With a pleasant expression on your face, give yourself a high five.

VARIATION

1. Tape a picture of yourself as a child to your mirror.
2. When you wake up in the morning and start your day, look at the picture and give it a compliment, send it love, blow a kiss to it, or give it a high five.
3. If you find yourself thinking something negative, look at the picture and ask, "Would I say such a thing to this child?" Send a kind gesture, such as a high five, instead.

JOURNAL PROMPT: List three things you love about your body and describe why you love those parts. How can you show your body more love?

Identify Your Triggers

When we identify who and what causes our triggers, it becomes easier to manage the way we respond when heavy emotions come up. When you can move past this trigger, that shadow aspect of you is no longer in control.

1. Choose one trigger to explore and respond to the following questions, while showing yourself kindness and compassion:

   - Who/what elicits that trigger within you?
   - How do you react when you experience that emotion? Do you shut down? Do you scream? Be specific.
   - How long has this triggered you? When was the first time you experienced this trigger?
   - Have you noticed any patterns with this trigger, whether from your past or watching other family members react this way?
   - What is a healthier way to manage your emotions when this trigger comes up?
   - How can you move through this feeling?
   - How would you respond differently if this trigger did not affect you?

2. Close this exercise by grounding your energy. Take a walk or run outside, walk barefoot in the grass, or do a meditation that helps you return to the present moment.

JOURNAL PROMPT: Are you holding a grudge or resentment toward a particular person or event? If so, describe it. How would you feel if this resentment no longer affected you?

Criticize Others

Allow yourself to freely speak your judgments and opinions of others out loud in a safe environment. Do this alone so that you can be fully present with these thoughts without worrying about having to hold back. Speaking your criticisms aloud helps you gain a better understanding of where you judge other people as well as yourself.

1. Set aside 5 to 10 minutes of time when you can be alone and where you will not be overheard.
2. During this time, speak your judgments aloud. Be completely uninhibited during this process.
3. Bring to mind different people, groups of people, or types of people. For each, identify what you feel about this person, type, or group. What emotions arise for you? What criticisms do you have?
4. Now turn it around. Ask yourself if any of these criticisms or judgments reflect how you feel about yourself.

JOURNAL PROMPT: How does your judgment of others reflect the way you feel about yourself? Do you place judgment on your body, emotions, behaviors, and/or actions? If so, why?

Be Useless

Make time in your day to literally "be useless." It is not necessary to be productive one hundred percent of the time. Give yourself space and time to sit back and rest with zero judgment and complete compassion for yourself as a human being.

1. Carve out a time to be unproductive. This could be a day, a whole weekend, or a few hours.

2. At the appointed time, fully immerse yourself in the experience of being useless.

3. Allow yourself this time to rest, zone out, and chill. This part is completely up to you, so do whatever you want as long as it is not work-related or "productive." Keep in mind that the goal is to be useless.

4. If judgment arises about being unproductive, question that inner critic. What makes you think it's not okay to do nothing?

JOURNAL PROMPT: Describe how you feel when others are useless or you think they are not doing anything productive with their lives. In what ways do you honor your own energy and allow yourself time to rest and recharge?

Draw Yourself

It's time to access your creativity and create your self-portrait. Grab some paper and drawing utensils or your tablet with your favorite art app. You can also paint or use magazine cut-outs. Whatever method you prefer will work.

1. Draw how you look. Draw what you feel. Draw what you see when you look in the mirror.

2. To help you get specific, ask yourself questions like: *How does this person dress? How does this person behave? How does this person speak? What does this person think?*

3. Review your work as you go to look for any missing aspects of yourself and add them in however you'd like.

4. When you feel that the portrait is complete, assess your drawing. What does it tell you about yourself?

JOURNAL PROMPT: What parts of yourself do you allow to be fully seen and expressed? What parts do you try to hide away? How are these aspects of you illustrated by your self-portrait?

Quality Alone Time

Spending time alone is not only an amazing form of self-care, but it can also offer you a great way to face any triggers that bring up feelings of loneliness, abandonment, vulnerability, lack of self-confidence, being unloved, etc. Intentional time alone without any distractions from other people, outside noise, or conversations allows you to *really* see yourself. Use this time to tend to yourself and your needs.

1. Set aside time to spend quality time alone. You can schedule this in your calendar, pick a weekend night, or just show up for yourself whenever you feel ready.

2. Make plans with just you! Pick something you enjoy doing, like baking or cooking, gardening, taking a bath, or walking in nature. Your options are virtually limitless.

3. When you're spending this time alone, intentionally seek out elevated states of emotions. If you feel like laughing, do so with gusto. Or if you feel like you could use a good crying session, let it all out. This is not a place for judgment or self-hatred, but rather awareness of how spending time alone really makes you feel.

JOURNAL PROMPT: Where are you putting yourself last? Where are you showing up for your goals, wishes, and desires? How do you expect others to treat you? How do you treat yourself?

Be Physically Powerful

On your healing journey, it's key to find ways to set boundaries, protect your peace, and feel confident. If you find any of these difficult, engaging in physical movements that make you feel stronger and more powerful may be what you need to face aspects of your shadow that don't allow you to exhibit these empowering behaviors. This sense of physical protection will cascade into other areas of your life. Check with a healthcare professional if you have any limitations that should be considered.

1. Determine what kind of physical movements you would like to try, such as punching, kicking, pushing, or lifting weights. Whatever movement requires you to move your body in strong, powerful ways works.

2. Search YouTube or other online sources for videos that teach the proper form for these movements.

3. As you practice these movements, be fully present in your body and visualize yourself taking up space in the world and powerfully defending your boundaries and yourself.

4. As you move, notice any aggression, resentment, anger, reservation, or apprehension that shows up for you. Notice if these emotions affect your ability to participate in this exercise.

JOURNAL PROMPT: In what areas and with what types of people do you find it difficult to maintain boundaries? Describe what it feels like to be empowered and safe in your own skin.

3

Prompts for Deep Exploration

The journal prompts in this chapter help you explore your shadow parts and cultivate a deeper understanding of yourself, and can help you fall in love with yourself. Explore each journal prompt in whatever order you feel called to. There is no right or wrong way to explore these, so let your intuition guide you toward what needs to be addressed during your specific shadow work session. To get the most from these prompts, be deeply honest with yourself.

SHADOW WORK GOALS: What do you most want to get out of shadow work? In what ways will your life transform because of it?

_____

_____

_____

_____

_____

_____

_____

_____

_____

_____

_____

_____

_____

_____

_____

_____

_____

_____

_____

_____

_____

ASKING FOR HELP: Describe how it feels when you ask someone for help. What about it is easy or difficult?

_____

_____

_____

_____

_____

_____

_____

_____

_____

_____

_____

_____

_____

_____

_____

_____

_____

_____

_____

_____

SEEKING SUPPORT: What types of people do you turn to for support? If no one can relate to your struggles, how do you feel about seeking professional help?

SOCIAL SUPPORT: Rate your social circle in terms of the amount of love and support you feel. Are you fully supported in these relationships or are there any weak bonds? How can you make changes?

AUTHENTIC SELF: How does it feel to be your authentic self around other people? When it comes to your closest relationships, which parts of yourself do you reveal or hide?

_____

_____

_____

_____

_____

_____

_____

_____

_____

_____

_____

_____

_____

_____

_____

_____

_____

_____

_____

_____

_____

_____

_____

_____

LOVE IT OR LOATHE IT: What types of people do you feel like you can truly be yourself around? Do they bring out aspects of you that you love or loathe? Describe how they help you be true to yourself, even if they bring out parts you don't like.

_____

_____

_____

_____

_____

_____

_____

_____

_____

_____

_____

_____

_____

_____

_____

_____

_____

_____

DISGUISES: Who or what groups of people do you wear a disguise around to feel like you fit in? What is your disguise covering up? Describe why you feel shame about these aspects of yourself.

SELF-ACCEPTANCE: Do you accept yourself for *all* of who you are? If not, what parts of you are too hard to accept?

INNER VOICE: Is your inner voice kind or critical? What does it say to you on a typical day? Who from your life does that inner voice resemble (parents, teachers, partners, etc.)?

_____

_____

_____

_____

_____

_____

_____

_____

_____

_____

_____

_____

_____

_____

_____

_____

_____

_____

_____

_____

_____

_____

BETRAYAL: When did you feel most betrayed? How old were you? Describe the situation and how it affected you.

BREAKING PROMISES: What's the biggest promise you made to yourself that you broke? Why did you break it? How do you feel about that? What might have been different if you had kept your promise?

BLAME: Describe a time when you blamed someone else for a negative outcome. What aspects of that situation might you have been partly responsible for?

VICTIM BLAMING: Do you blame yourself for a trauma that you experienced? If so, why? Did someone else blame you for it? What was their reasoning?

_____

_____

_____

_____

_____

_____

_____

_____

_____

_____

_____

_____

_____

_____

_____

_____

_____

_____

_____

_____

_____

BODY POSITIVITY: How comfortable do you feel in your body? List your ten best physical traits. If you would like to change something about yourself, what is it and why?

BOUNDARIES: What is one new boundary you should set to safeguard your well-being? How will you maintain this boundary with yourself and other people?

CHALLENGES: What is the most challenging aspect of your life right now? What are you learning from it? How can you grow from it?

BRAVERY: Describe someone you think is brave. What makes that person brave? How can your own bravery help and inspire others?

_____

_____

_____

_____

_____

_____

_____

_____

_____

_____

_____

_____

_____

_____

_____

_____

_____

_____

_____

_____

_____

_____

_____

_____

HOLIDAY MEMORIES: What are your most prominent childhood memories of holidays? Would you categorize them mostly as positive or negative? Why?

NEEDS: What did you need as a child but never receive? Why did you need those things? Why didn't you receive them?

COMPARISON: Do you generally feel less than, equal to, or better than others? Explore this deeper by describing why you might feel this way.

VALUES: What's most important to you in life? What are you morally passionate about? Describe whether you lead your life in alignment with these values. Do you surround yourself with people who have the same values? Why or why not?

CAREGIVERS' VALUES: What did your parents/caregivers value when you were growing up? Do you hold these values today or do they differ? How so?

GRATITUDE: What are you grateful for? Think about the past few days and describe five to ten things that you were happy about or pleased with, no matter how small.

EMOTIONS: Which emotions do you avoid feeling most often and why? Which do you engage with the most and why?

FAILURE AND SUCCESS: What does failure mean to you? What about success? When was the last time you felt like a failure? When did you feel successful?

FACING FAILURE: Think about something you failed at and felt ashamed for failing. What made these circumstances so terrible? If you witnessed someone else fail at the same thing, what would you say to help them feel better?

FEAR: In what areas of your life are you playing small or functioning with fear? Why are you allowing yourself to do this? How can you shift this?

_____

_____

_____

_____

_____

_____

_____

_____

_____

_____

_____

_____

_____

_____

_____

_____

_____

_____

_____

FORGIVENESS: Without reaching out to this person, think of someone from your past whom you can forgive. Remember, forgiveness does not mean you approve of anything they did or didn't do. What would you say to that person to free yourself of resentment?

SELF-DEPRECATION: What is the worst thing you have ever said to yourself? How can you make up for it? What acts of self-love can you implement into your life?

SELF-FORGIVENESS: What is one thing you need to forgive yourself for? Why have you been holding on to this? How would you feel if you released this shame or guilt?

_____

_____

_____

_____

_____

_____

_____

_____

_____

_____

_____

_____

_____

_____

_____

_____

_____

_____

_____

_____

INHERITED TRAITS: What are the worst traits you've noticed in your family? What are the best? Describe how these traits make you feel. Do you share these traits?

INJUSTICE: Do you speak up in the face of injustice or confrontation? Why or why not? How would it feel to do the opposite?

DEALING WITH HURT: How have you dealt with negative life events and painful experiences? What have you done about it? What would you change about how you deal with pain in the future?

_____

_____

_____

_____

_____

_____

_____

_____

_____

_____

_____

_____

_____

_____

_____

_____

_____

_____

_____

_____

_____

UNANSWERED QUESTIONS: What is a question you had as a child that you never got a real answer to? Do you still wonder about this? What would happen if you had the answer? Would this bring a sense of closure? Why or why not?

LONELINESS: Describe the time when you felt the most alone as well as the time when you felt most connected. What's similar and/or different about these instances?

LOVE: What is your definition of love? Do you show yourself this kind of love? If not, describe your own version of self-love.

_____

_____

_____

_____

_____

_____

_____

_____

_____

_____

_____

_____

_____

_____

_____

_____

_____

_____

_____

_____

_____

SELF-LOVE: In what area of your life do you not treat yourself with love? Why is that? How would a person who loves themselves treat themselves?

MENTAL HEALTH: What are the first things you notice about yourself when you realize that your mental health is struggling? How do you support yourself at these times?

MISCONCEPTIONS: What misconception do people have about you? How does that make you feel? Why do you think they see you that way?

_____

_____

_____

_____

_____

_____

_____

_____

_____

_____

_____

_____

_____

_____

_____

_____

_____

_____

_____

MISUNDERSTANDINGS: What might you misunderstand about how certain people behave toward you? What other reasons could there be for their behaviors?

SELF-WORTH: Describe how status and income affect your sense of self-worth. If finances do not play a part, what else brings you a sense of self-worth and how can you enhance those positive feelings?

_____

_____

_____

_____

_____

_____

_____

_____

_____

_____

_____

_____

_____

_____

_____

_____

_____

_____

_____

_____

MONEY: How did your family's relationship with money impact your view of making, spending, and saving money? Is your perspective aligned with scarcity or abundance? If scarcity, how might you change that?

SPECIAL TREATS: What was the last thing you purchased for yourself just because you wanted it? How did the purchase make you feel? If you could buy anything you wanted, what would it be?

FINANCIAL SECRETS: Should people be open about the amount of money they make? Why or why not? Did your parents/caregivers keep their income a secret from you and/or others? How has this impacted how open you are with finances?

MONEY SHAME: Do you believe there is shame in admitting that you want or need more money? If so, describe why the thought of not having enough money makes you feel ashamed.

MONEY TRANSPARENCY: Write about a time when you wanted to "show" someone that you had money (or that you don't have enough and are struggling). Did you want to flaunt this or just allude to it? Why did you feel compelled to do this?

NEGATIVE THOUGHTS: What negative thoughts are you feeding your subconscious? What is the source of each of these thoughts? Brainstorm some positive thoughts to replace them.

PAINFUL EMOTIONS: How does it feel to allow yourself to experience painful emotions? Describe any resistance around processing your emotions and experiences.

PEOPLE PLEASING: Are you a people pleaser? In what ways do you show up for others but not for yourself? Why do you do this?

SELF-CARE: Describe how you take care of yourself. When you take this time for yourself, how do you feel before, during, and after?

POSITIVE FEELINGS: Write in detail about the people, experiences, and commitments that triggered positive feelings, energy, and emotions for you in the last twelve months.

REGRETS: Imagine for a moment that you are at the end of your life. What is your biggest regret? Brainstorm ways in which you can address change so you no longer anticipate these regrets.

RELATIONSHIP BOUNDARIES: Do you have healthy boundaries in your relationships? Which could benefit from stronger boundaries? Describe how you do or don't respect the boundaries of others.

UNKIND BEHAVIOR: When was the last time you were mean or hurtful? Why did you behave that way? Did you do anything to shift this? What can you do today to make someone smile?

RELATIONSHIP RELEASE: Which relationships in your life no longer serve you? What would happen if you released these relationships?

LETTING GO: What thought, belief, behavior, situation, and/or physical object is no longer serving you? Are you willing to release it? Why or why not?

REPARENTING: In what ways can you reparent yourself today? In other words, how can you meet the needs of your inner child that weren't met when you were growing up? How would your younger self feel if they had received this same treatment?

REPLENISHMENT: What do you need to do to replenish yourself? How do you recover after a hard day at work? After getting physically hurt? After an argument?

RESPONSIBILITY: In what ways are you being mature and responsible in your healing and growth journey?

_____

_____

_____

_____

_____

_____

_____

_____

_____

_____

_____

_____

_____

_____

_____

_____

_____

_____

_____

VULNERABILITY: Do you allow yourself to be vulnerable in your relationships? Why or why not? How vulnerable are you in your romantic relationship? What about your friendships?

PUTTING YOURSELF FIRST: In what ways are you putting yourself last? Why? What does putting yourself first look like? What would happen if you did that?

_____

_____

_____

_____

_____

_____

_____

_____

_____

_____

_____

_____

_____

_____

_____

_____

_____

_____

_____

_____

_____

_____

SELF-IMPROVEMENT: What aspects of yourself would you like to improve and why? Has anyone ever suggested that you should try to improve in this area? If so, how did that make you feel?

SELF-KINDNESS: In what ways have you been punishing yourself? Brainstorm ways to be kinder to yourself.

UNWORTHY OF LOVE: Do you feel unworthy of being loved by others and/or yourself? What steps can you take to give yourself a healthy sense of self-worth? How would life be different if you felt worthy?

_____

_____

_____

_____

_____

_____

_____

_____

_____

_____

_____

_____

_____

_____

_____

_____

_____

SEXUALITY: Do you embrace yourself as a sexual being or are you embarrassed by your sexuality or desires? Explain why.

SHAME: What times have you felt most ashamed in your life? What caused the shame?

_____

_____

_____

_____

_____

_____

_____

_____

_____

_____

_____

_____

_____

_____

_____

_____

_____

_____

_____

_____

UNWANTED TRAITS: What do you think are the worst traits a person can have? Can you think of a time when you have demonstrated these traits?

TOXIC BEHAVIORS: In what situations are you overly negative or manipulative? Where do you stir up drama? Describe the last time you expressed any type of toxic behavior in your close relationships and how the outcome made you feel.

TRIGGER STATEMENTS: What is one statement someone could say to you that would instantly set you off, causing you to react in a negative way? Why does this statement have this effect on you?

TRIGGER QUALITIES: What common qualities are shared by the people, situations, or things that trigger you? Do you share any of these qualities? Remember, we are only bothered by something if it is part of our shadow.

WEAKNESS: What makes you feel weak? Is it asking for help, being unable to meet a goal, or something else? Brainstorm the initial source of this feeling.

LESSONS ABOUT YOU: Who taught you about who you are as you were growing up? Does this resonate with how you feel about yourself today?

WORTHINESS: What regularly triggers feelings in you that you are "not good enough" or that cause you to feel less than others? Why do you think this is?

NEGATIVE EVENTS: In what way might past negative events affect your current relationships? What steps can you take to rectify this and approach your relationships with a more positive outlook?

FUTURE YOU: What are you creating for your future self? How much money do you want to earn? What would your most intimate relationship look like? What type of environment will you be living in? What do the supportive relationships around you feel like?

ABOUT THE AUTHORS

 **VALERIE INEZ** is a Houston-based writer, intuitive, healer, and shadow work guide. As a Scorpio, she is comfortable diving deep into the shadows to bring the darkness into the light. She helps her clients rise from the ashes, find their inner magic, and step into their divine power. Valerie enjoys reading, writing, spending time with her children, exploring nature, and finding new ways to connect to the Universe.

 **LATHA JAY** is a spiritual manifestation coach who blends modern knowledge with traditional wisdom. She integrates what she has learned through life experiences into various healing modalities to teach people to shift perceptions, manifest, and live happier lives. She is passionate about guiding clients through lifestyle and mindset modifications to transform their lives into a new experience of happiness, freedom, and love. When not working with clients, writing, spending time with her family, or building courses, Latha spends her days learning from others, farming, and persistently maintaining a beginner's mindset in everything she does.

Hi there,

We hope you enjoyed *Shadow Work Journal for Self-Love*. If you have any questions or concerns about your book, or have received a damaged copy, please contact customerservice@penguinrandomhouse.com. We're here and happy to help.

Also, please consider writing a review on your favorite retailer's website to let others know what you thought of the book!

Sincerely,
The Zeitgeist Team

EXOPOLITICS

EXOPOLITICS

POLITICS, GOVERNMENT, AND LAW
IN THE UNIVERSE

A Treatise

ALFRED LAMBREMONT WEBRE
J.D. M.Ed.

Forewords by

DR. COURTNEY BROWN
Director, The Farsight Institute

and

PAUL DAVIDS
Executive Producer, *ROSWELL*

Edited by Andrew D. Basiago

Universebooks
Vancouver, B.C.
CANADA

For copyright licenses, please contact:
Universebooks
www.universebooks.com

Library and Archives Canada Cataloguing in Publication

Webre, Alfred Lambremont, 1942-

Exopolitics: politics, government, and law in the Universe: a treatise/ Alfred Lambremont Webre; forewords by Courtney Brown, Ph.D. and Paul Davids; edited by Andrew D. Basiago.

ISBN 0-9737663-0-1

1. Life on other planets. 2. Political science. 3. Outer space. I. Title.

QB54.W42 2005   320.999   C2005-901996-4

Printed on 100% Post-Consumer Recycled Paper.

Cover Image: *Giant Mothership Entering Time Door* © and courtesy of James Neff.

Printed in Canada

Other Books by Alfred Lambremont Webre

The Age of Cataclysm (New York: G.P. Putnam's Sons, 1974)
(New York: Berkeley Medallion, 1975); (Capricorn Books, 1975)
(Tokyo: Ugaku Sha, 1975)
The Levesque Cases (Ontario: PSP Books, 1990)
Earth Changes: A Spiritual Approach (Universebooks, 2000)
Recovery: A Personal Journey (Universebooks, 2000)

DEDICATION

**For all generations – past, present, and future –
and for gaga**

We cast this message into the Cosmos... Of the 200 billion stars in the Milky Way galaxy, some – perhaps many – may have inhabited planets and space-faring civilizations. If one such civilization intercepts Voyager and can understand these recorded contents, here is our message: We are trying to survive our time so we may live into yours. We hope some day, having solved the problems we face, to join a community of Galactic Civilizations. This record represents our hope and our determination and our goodwill in a vast and awesome Universe.

– President Jimmy Carter's official statement placed on the Voyager spacecraft for its trip outside our solar system, June 16th, 1977

Contents

What Others are Saying
about EXOPOLITICS

NICK POPE
UFO Desk Officer, UK Ministry of Defense, 1991-1994

UFOs have been seen throughout human history. Witnesses have included police officers, pilots, and even presidents. The phenomenon has been the subject of scientific study, and has been investigated by the governments and the military of many countries around the world. The evidence is compelling and includes UFOs sighted by pilots, simultaneously tracked on radar, and anomalous radiation readings taken where UFOs have been seen to land. While there is much controversy over many UFO sightings, these facts are not disputed and have been confirmed by official documents released in response to various Freedom of Information Act requests in recent years.

Although the study of UFOs is fascinating in itself, there is a bigger picture. Most scientists in relevant fields now believe that we are likely to share the Universe with a myriad of other life forms. Frank Drake, the scientist who originated the concept of using radio telescopes to search for evidence of extraterrestrial life, estimated that our own galaxy, the Milky Way, might contain 10,000 intelligent, technological civilizations. Recent scientific discoveries, including those relating to extra-solar planets, have led Drake and others to conclude that they may have underestimated the figure considerably. How then should we view humanity in such a crowded Universe?

This is where Exopolitics comes in. I confidently predict that it's a word we'll be hearing more of over the next few years. It relates to the study of humanity not just as inhabitants of Planet Earth but in the wider context of our position in a Universe that we share with other civilizations. Racism, nationalism, and self-interest may suggest that humanity is not yet ready to deal in open contact with other civilizations. How can we hope to get along with other civilizations when we cannot get along with each other? And yet, for all our problems, there are hopeful signs that people are taking a less insular perspective. A growing spiritual awareness and cross-cultural concern about issues such as global warming and the weaponization of space suggest that humanity is capable of taking a wider perspective. This mindset goes to the heart of Exopolitics.

Alfred Webre can be regarded as the founding father of Exopolitics as a field of human inquiry. His involvement with the study of the UFO phenomenon includes work with the Carter Administration and with the prestigious Stanford Research Institute, which are impressive credentials in this most controversial of emerging sciences. His book, *Exopolitics*, gives an overview of the field and offers a blueprint for humanity as it moves toward taking its place on a wider stage. It is a roadmap to the stars.

ROBERT O. DEAN

Command Sergeant-Major, USAF (Retired); Intelligence Analyst (Cosmic Top Secret clearance), Supreme Headquarters Allied Powers Europe (SHAPE)

It's been 40 years now since I first became aware of the reality of the extraterrestrial presence on Planet Earth. Since that experience, my life has never been quite the same. A fire was ignited within my very being. I continued to learn, to seek, and to know more and more about what I later came to understand is the most important issue in human history. The issue is not that we are not alone, but that we have *never* been alone.

I was to learn that the human race has had, and continues to have, an intimate interrelationship with several incredibly advanced intelligent races from other planets, solar systems, and star systems within our galaxy – and that this relationship has been underway for several thousand years.

These star-traveling civilizations are as far beyond humans on Planet Earth as modern America is beyond the head hunting tribes of New Guinea. This is primarily why disclosure has not taken place – and why disclosure is not contemplated by the unacknowledged US government agencies that oversee this great secret.

I have always proclaimed that an understanding and acceptance of the reality that we are not alone would bring with it an expansion of human consciousness that will transform the human species and guarantee our survival. The whole story is literally mind-boggling. The truth is shocking, disturbing, frightening, and socially and theologically explosive. In my later, more mature years, I have almost come to understand why the secret government has kept a lid on this greatest secret of all time for so long, and why they are so frightened to open Pandora's Box.

You see, we simply cannot open Pandora's Box just a little bit. Once we open it, nothing will ever be the same. A major new paradigm will come crashing in and our old world will come crashing down. Religion, society, politics – all will be utterly changed forever. Obviously, this is what the world's governments fear.

The final reality is that the story must be told and will be told. *Exopolitics* is a logical, rational, and scholarly attempt to clarify and present to the world the structure of an existing reality that can become a valuable tool in educating and expanding human consciousness. To this effort, I commend Alfred Webre and other members of the Institute for Cooperation in Space (ICIS) for their courage and dedication. I give my full support and encouragement to this endeavor, and I pray that it succeeds. If we ever mature as a race, we must recognize our extended family and reach out to them with courage and fellowship. *Exopolitics* can show us the way.

FATHER JOHN ROSSNER, Ph.D., D.Sc., D.Litt.
President, International Institute for Integral Human Sciences;
Adjunct Professor, Religion and Culture, Concordia University, Montreal, Quebec, Canada

Alfred Lambremont Webre defines "Exopolitics" as a new discipline for understanding "Universe society" through its politics and government. In such terms, it would "…posit that the truest conception of our earthly circumstance may be that we are on an isolated planet in the midst of a populated, evolving, highly organized inter-planetary, inter-galactic, multi-dimensional Universe society."

This statement – whether one "believes" ETI or contactee reports or not – should be highly interesting to historians of religion and culture. The history of human cultures, East and West, ancient and modern, is replete with accounts of encounters with "beings from space worlds," interacting with humans for varied purposes throughout the ages. One might well ask why the imagination of so many in cultures not in contact with one another have come up with, and been captivated by, this repetitive "myth"—*one that often defies their accepted "logic."*

New paradigms of science, and new models for understanding a "multi-dimensional Universe" – in which consciousness, intuition, and "non-local communications" are realities of common experience – are already widespread today.

In this context, Webre's championship of the new discipline of Exopolitics is a very credible academic and scientific pursuit. His extraordinary qualifications as a former researcher and a futurist at SRI's Center for the Study of Social Policy, and as an advisor to government on this subject, contributes to this study's significance as a contribution to knowledge at the beginning of the 21st century.

RABBI DR. NATHAN LOPES CARDOZO
Author, Scholar, Lecturer; Dean, The David Cardozo School, Machon Ohr Aharon

As our globe gets smaller and smaller, our eyes start to focus more and more on the many worlds around us. It is not just that we need more physical space for ourselves, but also existentially. We are contemporaries of God and we are duty-bound to reveal more of His greatness. Consequently, we must ask ourselves, how shall we discover more and more of Him? Alfred Webre's book makes us realize that this may be possible in ways we did not imagine some years ago.

ROBERT L. NICHOL
Filmmaker, Educator; Producer, *Star Dreams: Exploring the Mystery of the Crop Circles* (award-winning documentary)

Alfred Webre's treatise, *Exopolitics*, bodes well for those of us interested in the next step we must take as a species to evolve as universal beings.

Here again, much will be made about the cover-up of our universal heritage, but, in truth, we need to move beyond that controversy to an awareness of the global significance of our arising consciousness and our realization of a greater cosmic reality. This, so aptly communicated in Alfred's work, is the needed direction to take and the role that must be played by humanity at this time. *Exopolitics* is an inspiration, providing for me a greater understanding of my own evolving comprehension of the extraterrestrial presence and our place in the Universe.

URI GELLER
World-Renowned Psychic and Best-Selling Author, www.urigeller.com

I urge everyone who has an open mind to read this exciting and fascinating book, which is so thought provoking that it breaks all barriers of logic and rationalism and makes ancient theories tangible and real.

LINDA MOULTON HOWE
Reporter, Editor, Earthfiles.com; Science/Environment News Contributor, Clear Channel's Premiere Radio Networks

Exopolitics – Politics, Government, and Law in the Universe. That is a bold book title, given that most of this planet's human population is taught that we are a unique life form alone in the Universe. But author Alfred Lambremont Webre speaks as a futurist with a background at the Center for the Study of Social Policy at Stanford Research Institute, and as the current International Director of the Institute for Cooperation in Space.

Alfred Webre makes many bold assertions in this book that will provoke readers to argue that his statements are opinion and speculation, not fact. Perhaps at the same time, readers will also feel an intuitive resonance with his premise that Earth life cannot be the only life in the vast Cosmos. He points out that a Gallup poll in 1996 "showed that 72% of the US adult population believes there is some form of extraterrestrial life, and 45% believes the Earth has already been visited by extraterrestrial beings."

Anticipating a time in the future when banner headlines will proclaim, "We are Not Alone!" Webre promises that "Transformation of human society will occur when we reach a Universe-sensitive mass. With approximately 45% of Earth's population now extraterrestrial-conscious, can critical mass be far behind?"

Despite many controversial contentions, including the author's thesis that the Earth is in a political quarantine enforced by Someone Else's universal law, *Exopolitics* forces the reader to wonder what exactly would happen if this round of humankind, with all its government-controlled perceptions, was finally faced with the presence of ETs?

Exopolitics emerges at a time when astronomers are finding many planets beyond Earth and quantum string astrophysicists describe even other universes parallel to this one. If the Cosmos is filled with life, then multiple life forms and their various agendas would inevitably mean "social food fights," as Mr. Webre describes it, and would require government and law in the Universe.

HONORABLE PAUL T. HELLYER

Minister of National Defense under Canadian Prime Minister Lester B. Pearson; Deputy Prime Minister of Canada under Prime Minister Pierre Trudeau

Alfred Lambremont Webre's odyssey into the realm of life in the vast Universe surrounding Planet Earth is indeed a fascinating journey if you read it with an open mind. He postulates a Universe that includes many planets sustaining life more advanced than our own – all subject to universal governance based on the rule of law.

Earth, he suggests, is an exception. Rather than being the center of the Universe, as our ancestors believed, we are the black sheep of the interplanetary community. We have been "quarantined" and isolated from the "highly organized, interplanetary, inter-galactic multidimensional Universe society," presumably because our culture has been strongly influenced by rogue planetary leadership personified in the story of the Garden of Eden.

To end the "quarantine," Earthlings must advance morally and spiritually, while re-establishing connection with inter-planetary society. Until recently, we didn't have the technology to do the latter, but increasingly we do. Meanwhile, visits from our extra-planetary neighbours present opportunities for peaceful communication and collaboration.

Webre posits that some UFOs are natural phenomena, while some are top-secret military aircraft, but that others are quite real. He maintains that knowledge of their existence is being suppressed by military intelligence organizations in the five English-speaking countries known as the so-called "Echelon" group – the United Kingdom, the United States, Canada, Australia, and New Zealand.

For me, this is the least credible of the author's assertions. I strongly suspect that the US military holds information it has not revealed, but I very much doubt that it has shared this knowledge with its intelligence partners – certainly not Canada. The US only shares information with other governments when it is in its own best interests to do so.

Webre states that the alleged disinformation campaign about UFOs is due to the close relationship between the military and industry, the so-called "military-industrial complex" that President Dwight David Eisenhower warned us about in his farewell address. They are the chief beneficiaries of the oil economy. Tapping into the knowledge of the Universe would ultimately lead us to higher forms of energy that would be ecologically sustainable, but that would make the oil economy irrelevant.

God-fearing people will be relieved to know that there is nothing in Webre's thesis, despite the considerable mind-stretch, that denies their fundamental beliefs. If there were, I would not be a party to it. Webre states, "Reunion with Universe civilizations will bring a closer relationship with God. The most advanced scientific reality in all creation is that God is Source."

To turn us in the direction of re-unification with the rest of creation the author is proposing a "Decade of Contact" – an "era of openness, public hearings, publicly funded research, and education about extraterrestrial reality." That could be just the antidote the world needs to end its greed-driven, power-centered madness.

JEANE MANNING
Author, *The Coming Energy Revolution: The Search for Free Energy*

Alfred Lambremont Webre makes a logical case for the assertion that "most of the story modern human beings have been told about Earth and its outer space environs is wrong." He presents the hypothesis that Earth is a quarantined planet in a populated, evolving, highly organized interplanetary, inter-galactic, multi-dimensional Universe society of life-bearing planets – and that the quarantine, which probably had a spiritual cause, may soon be ending. He argues that before being invited "in," however, our society will have to kick its perpetual war habit.

His brilliant treatise, *Exopolitics*, forms a conceptual bridge between the familiar, locked-in, consensually limited thinking of our terrestrial society and the expanded options that humanity will enjoy in what Webre calls "Universe Society." In light of my chosen areas of interest and advocacy – especially, socio-economic, environmental, geopolitical, and spiritual awareness issues related to truly paradigm-shifting energy inventions – I find that, for me, his insights ring true.

Exopolitics fits conceptually within the models provided by frontier science that envision an endlessly creative Universe. Instead of the 20th century model, in which entropy rules and the Universe is dying and will run down someday, dissident physicists, such as those aligned with the international Natural Philosophers' Alliance, point to ongoing creation as well as dissolution as a principle underlying how the Universe is structured.

As a journalist who has interviewed heretical physicists and engineers for two decades now on various continents, I have witnessed the testing of at least a few prototypes of non-conventional converters that undeniably tap into some previously unrecognized source of energy in the Universe. I've met well-educated researchers who, over the years, have put together laboratories containing used or built-from-scratch equipment that would have cost more than a million dollars; these were not stereotypical "garage inventors." Some of them have the benefit of advice from seasoned scientists who are open to seriously investigating new (or rediscovered) ether-based science.

They refer to the new science as "zero-point energy," a term that is more easily accepted in today's physics vernacular than the supposedly disproved concept of "the ether." Relatively few academics (and even fewer members of the public) know that the famous Michelson-Morley experiment of 1887, that attempted to measure the Earth's velocity, through the ether, and didn't, was conducted on the basis of a mistaken assumption about the qualities of "the ether," or background energy of the Universe. Later experiments by Dayton Miller and others yielded a truer picture, but that is beyond the scope of this review. The website www.aetherometry.com presents evidence, derived from experiments by Dr. Paulo and Alexandra Correa of Canada, for a universal, mass-free energy.

Having majored in sociology rather than the hard sciences at university,

I rely on experts with the requisite technical background to interpret developments in the new science for me and to judge the merits of energy-generating inventions. My interest is in the social implications of clean energy sources that have enough energy density to free humanity from its perceived need for carbon-based fuels and nuclear fission. An even stronger passion is the spiritual implications of the new energy, which sheds light on the age-old insight of the great sages and mystics that "everything is interconnected."

On a technical level, the search to understand an emerging science related to abundant energy sources challenges independent scientists around the world. In some cases, their energy-generating inventions seem to "have a mind of their own" and will, practically speaking, most likely be unreliable until the researchers have more complete knowledge about the etheric energy (or other energy fields) that their "cosmic windmills" seem to be tapping into.

Meanwhile, financial, corporate, and political interest groups actively oppose independent efforts, so much so that in some places, the relentless search for understanding has gone underground. I've interviewed credible researchers who report vandalized laboratories, threats on their lives, or, more often, charming con men that promise funding that never materializes. At best, they waste months of an inventor's time in meetings and unmet promises of funding. At worst, inventors have found themselves enmeshed in financial difficulties or even put in jail after innocently believing such individuals. We can only speculate as to who or what unleashes such troublemakers onto gifted but vulnerable inventors.

I have seen their revolutionary energy converters tap into a cosmic source of energy and put out useable electric or thermal power for hours at a time. Of course, these are only the crude, initial efforts of a new technology. More sophisticated versions are rumored to reside in laboratories associated with the "Unacknowledged Special Access Programs" (USAPs) of the military-industrial-intelligence complex.

I have witnessed demonstrations of various types of inventions, such as solid-state arrangements of magnets and circuits, in which the Coefficient of Performance was greater than "1" – where more output was achieved than was invested from any recognizable power source. With a few exceptions, such as the Patterson Power Cell, these demonstrations were done in private. Shadowy groups have on numerous occasions threatened inventors of revolutionary energy devices, and over the years this has engendered a climate of fear. As a result of this fear, as well as competitive patenting, financial, and commercial factors, inventors have become secretive and somewhat averse to publicity.

Despite these social constraints, "new energy" research and development is progressing. Its progress has been halting and painfully slow, because, in my opinion, the prevailing worldview on Earth cannot embrace the concept of abundance. The prevailing view is that our species is doomed to perpetual warfare over scarce resources. There is ample evidence that ordinary humans prefer to be cooperative neighbours instead of competent soldiers, but that fact is too often overlooked.

The halting progress includes new hydrogen energy production. The website www.lenr-canr.org contains numerous scientific papers about remarkable experimental results, including the transmutation of elements. General discussions for experimenters in all areas of new energy can be found on the JLN Labs website. A source of breaking news is www.zpenergy.com.

Exopolitics states that we, the human race, are collectively the exo-government, the planetary Universe society. This is also the position taken by the emerging grassroots movement that is pursuing new energy research and development. That movement is in its infancy, but an organization called the New Energy Movement, at www.newenergymovement.org, is dedicated to nurturing and sustaining it.

I highly recommend Alfred Lambremont Webre's new book, *Exopolitics*. It inspires hope for a better future, one in which humanity progresses beyond its present addictions to petroleum and war, and beyond its resistance to beneficial change, toward a higher level of spiritual awareness. My own experiences validate his assertion that the Universe is ultimately a spiritual domain.

 MICHAEL MANNION

Co-Founder, The Mindshift Institute; Author, *Project Mindshift: The Re-Education of the American Public Concerning Extraterrestrial Life*

Human understanding of the extraterrestrial phenomenon has evolved gradually over the past half-century. At first, there were arguments about whether the UFO-ET phenomenon was real or not. Next, the discussion moved to an exploration of the nature and purpose of the phenomenon.

Today, a conversation is beginning about initiating conscious human interaction with the life forms – the expressions of Nature – that we are calling "extraterrestrials."

Exopolitics: Politics, Government, and Law in the Universe is an exciting new book by Alfred Webre, a former futurist at the Stanford Research Institute, advisor to the Carter Administration on the extraterrestrial question, and Fulbright scholar, who received his law degree from Yale. At present, he is the International Director of the Institute for Cooperation in Space and founder of the No Weapons in Space Campaign. He is an activist working to prevent the weaponization of space and to transform our economy from one based on war to one based on peace and sustainability.

This fascinating book introduces readers to the subject of Exopolitics, which the author defines as "how a highly populated and regulated Universe governs itself," as well as to the existence of an organized interstellar "Universe society." Webre envisions possible conscious contact between Earth society and Universe society in the near future. This direct contact can only occur if humanity itself, not merely individual human beings, heals and undergoes a transformation.

In Webre's words, "The transformation starts within each of us; for we ourselves are the Universe transformation... We are the new universal human being." To achieve such a radical shift in our existence will require an open mind and a fearless willingness to let go of long-standing errors that are deeply embedded in our religions and science. Adherence to these erroneous views blocks our ability to understand the true nature of the Universe and how it functions.

The central aim of Exopolitics is to create a mass awareness of the fact that we live in a Universe composed of many organized civilizations. How does the author think that this can be accomplished? He proposes launching a "Decade of Contact," a period of openness, public hearings, publicly funded research, and education about the reality of extraterrestrial civilization and our connection to it.

Webre believes that Earth has been placed under "quarantine" by the Universe society but that there may now be an opening to change that status. His social activism is an example of what humanity needs to do to help end this quarantine. In his view, "In a Universe society, love rather than conflict is the central organizing principle among advanced societies." Unfortunately, on our planet, war is presently the organizing principle.

Take the time to listen to the message of *Exopolitics*. We all have a lot of work to do so that humanity can re-enter the cosmic community. Remember – you are the transformation that is needed to make this possibility a reality.

R. LEO SPRINKLE, Ph.D.
Counseling Psychologist; Professor Emeritus, University of Wyoming; Ufologist, Author

Any review of a scholarly work should address three questions: What is the stated goal of the author? How well does the author meet that goal? How does the book contribute to the literature of that discipline or special field?

The reader of a review should be given not only an intellectual assessment of the book, but also some insights into the author's intents and achievements, as perceived by the reviewer. Thus, the reader of the review can determine the bias of the reviewer and then decide whether to buy and/ or read the book.

The author of the book that you are about to read, *Exopolitics*, both educates and exhorts the reader to accept a bold and optimistic view of Earth and humanity. Well written, and well edited, the book explores the status of an isolated planet that is ready to join the cosmic community – "Universe society."

The author, Alfred Lambremont Webre, has advanced degrees in law and applied psychology. He offers his readers the results of many professional activities, including his work as a futurist at Stanford Research Institute. In 1977, he directed a project to develop an extraterrestrial (ET) communication proposal for the White House staff during President Jimmy Carter's administration.

Exopolitics provides an outline, or a model, for evaluating the current status and possible future of humanity. The stated goal is to provide a bridge between the current concept of Earth as an isolated planet and the future concept of Earth as a member of cosmic cultures, in a multidimensional Universe society.

Webre prepares the reader not only for changes in political "realities," but also for changes in scientific "realities." He emphasizes the principle of a holographic Universe. Both spiritual and material dimensions are ONE. Thus, spiritual and ethical, as well as scientific and technical, development, are signs of a planetary society that is ready for universal "reunion" in politics, government, and law.

Webre addresses a variety of questions: Is the story of the Garden of Eden a reflection of human origins in a cosmic context? Is Earth isolated because of quarantine by ET societies? Is humanity's history of violence – and current plans for military weapons in space – a significant factor in any quarantine by ET societies? Was there a rebellion by Earth's "gods," or governors, against the administrators of a larger cosmic community? Is the UFO phenomenon an indication of the strategy of an ET program? Does the Disclosure Project represent the means by which humanity formally recognizes the ET presence?

The author offers the concepts of "reflectivity" and "dimensionality" as methods by which humans become aware of higher consciousness and higher truth. Thus, both external (empirical) and internal (intuitive) methods are emphasized for exploring and evaluating truth.

For example, Webre uses the results of various public opinion polls as evidence to support dual hypotheses: Most adults are aware of both the ET presence and the UFO cover-up. Approximately half of US adults agree with the statement that ETs are visiting Earth, and more than half agree with the statement that governmental officials are withholding information about UFO reports.

Webre states: "A transformational Exobiology, Exoarcheology, and Exopolitics would construct a bridge of knowledge and relationship with advanced civilizations in the Universe." He calls for a Decade of Contact to prepare humanity for its alignment with Universe society.

In the reviewer's opinion, the author has done well in describing his goal, which is to present a model of Universe politics, and an approach by which humanity might align itself with the law and governance of a Universe society.

Has the author done well in meeting that goal? The reviewer recognizes that there can be a variety of evaluations, depending upon the attitudes of any reader.

The general reader might ask: How does the author know about Universe laws and government? Observation? Intuition? Information from ET societies?

Persons of "enlightened" views (from meditation, UFO and ET encounters, and advanced education) are likely to applaud as well as agree with Webre. Persons with "practical" concerns (e.g., job security, skepticism about intellectuals, and fear of "aliens") are not likely to read the book or react to the model. Persons with certain affiliations or "special interests" (e.g., scientism, religiosity, and covert operations) are likely to discount the model and reject the book.

Perhaps the current "game" will continue, in which the dominant culture maintains that "logical positivism" is the method and "physical evidence" is the measure of the method. If current conditions continue, then the UFO cover-up will continue, and the dominant culture will continue to deny the ET presence.

Webre argues that conditions, however, are changing. There are a variety of Earth conditions (e.g., pollution, global warming, and extinction of plants and animals) and a variety of human concerns (e.g., wars, cultural and religious conflicts, the gap between the rich and poor, and suppression of free energy technologies) that calls out for a new view of Earth and a new view of humanity.

Does the model of *Exopolitics* provide that perspective? How does the book *Exopolitics* contribute to the literature on Exopolitics?

The literature on Exopolitics can be grouped into four categories:

(1) Statements from writers of channeled messages from extraterrestrial (ET) or extra-dimensional (ED) entities, which describe ET or multidimensional communities;

(2) Reports from persons who describe encounters with ET/ED beings, and the messages from the beings about their worlds;

(3) Reports from persons who describe travels to other planets, or dimensions, and their observations of those communities;

(4) Comments from writers who analyze statements (e.g., "science fiction," speculation, and UFO/ET experiences) about various topics of Exopolitics.

This review cannot summarize the vast literature of ET contact (consider the Vedic traditions, the writings of Zecharia Sitchin, and the Old and New Testament), but it can give a few examples of recent writings for comparison with *Exopolitics*.

Members of the current scientific community usually focus on the physical and biological conditions that are needed for life to emerge on other (distant) planets. They may be supportive of SETI (the Search for Extraterrestrial Intelligence), but they seldom view UFO reports as an indication of ET visitation.

That gap between many scientists and most UFO investigators may be narrowing. For example, a recent article that explores the ET hypothesis – "Inflation-Theory Implications for Extraterrestrial Visitation," *Journal of the British Interplanetary Society*, vol. 58, 2005, pp. 43-50) was written by

James Deardorff, Bernard Haisch, Bruce Maccabee, and Hal E. Puthoff, who are mainstream scientists as well as UFO investigators.

Few psychologists and psychiatrists have participated in UFO research. The death of John Mack, M.D. in 2004, however, was the subject of several editorials, including Stephen Basset's "Exopolitics" column in the December-January 2005 edition of *UFO* magazine, pp. 16-18. Dr. Mack, a professor of psychiatry at Harvard University, had authored two books on UFO "abductees," and founded the Program for Extraordinary Experience Research (PEER).

Philip Krapf, a former news editor for the *Los Angeles Times*, has described his visits aboard ships of an ET civilization and their plans for contact with nations on Earth.

Courtney Brown, Ph.D., a professor of political science, has described his sessions of remote viewing, and his analysis of the political structure of an ET civilization.

C.B. "Scott" Jones, Ph.D. convened a group of international speakers in 1995, at a conference called When Cosmic Cultures Meet. The purpose of the conference, held in Washington, D.C., was to prepare both the public and government officials for possible disclosure of the ET presence.

The Disclosure Project, directed by Steven Greer, M.D., has videotaped testimony from hundreds of former military and government officials about their knowledge of the UFO cover-up.

Michael Salla, Ph.D., author of *Exopolitics: Political Implications of the Extraterrestrial Presence*, has reviewed international politics as influenced by the ET presence. He attempts to evaluate the levels of evidence for various aspects of the "politics of Exopolitics."

Paul von Ward, author of *Gods, Genes, and Consciousness*, analyzes evidence from various sources (archeological, cultural, genetic, historical, and technical knowledge) that ABs (Advanced Beings) have helped humans to establish Earth civilizations. His focus on "religious" traditions, and "scientific" traditions, provides an analysis of factors that sustain wars and other conflicts among cultures and nations. He offers an approach to ease the conflicts between different cultures with different "gods."

Ida M. Kannenberg has authored a fourth book, *Reconciliation*, with the assistance of high-level entities, THOTH and TRES. She analyzes the argument that humanity is spiritually ready to reassess its relationship with other levels of cosmic consciousness.

Lisette Larkins has authored three books on her communications with

ETs, emphasizing that anyone can communicate, telepathically, with extraterrestrial beings.

These brief examples indicate that a wide array of literature is available for any reader who wishes to evaluate the contribution of Webre and his model of Exopolitics.

If the reader of the review has doubts about intuitive processes for apprehending "truth," then the book, *Power Versus Force*, by David R. Hawkins, M.D., Ph.D., can provide an empirical method for assessing levels of consciousness or calibrating levels of truth.

If you have doubts about the UFO cover-up, then *UFOs and the National Security State*, a history by Richard Dolan, can provide the historical information needed to accept the reality of the ET presence and the UFO cover-up.

In my opinion, the author of this volume, Alfred Lambremont Webre, has presented to readers a small package that contains a huge gift – a new vision of humanity's place in the Cosmos. Most books about Exopolitics are written from the perspective of humanity, or from the perspective of the individual writer.

Webre has provided a perspective of universal law and government that rises above the mundane politics of humanity and Earth, and views humans not as Planetary Persons but as Cosmic Citizens.

When the reader is ready, his *Exopolitics* provides an individual and collective blueprint for developing a social structure on Earth that assists humanity, in a Decade of Contact, to join and participate in Universe society.

BRIAN O'LEARY, Ph.D.

Former NASA Astronaut; Founder, New Energy Movement; Author, *Re-Inventing the Earth: New Energy Sources, Future Sciences* and *Search for Extraterrestrial Life in the Universe*

Exopolitics explores a possible – and, if true, very important – cosmic view that the Universe is governed by advanced beings in higher spiritual and physical space, of which most of us on Earth are not aware or barely aware. According to this view, a long time ago, powerful Earthlings rebelled against the universal order, and we all got quarantined, driven away, temporarily, from the Garden of Eden, cut off from the richness of the interplanetary culture. Alfred Webre argues that we might be getting closer to the time of revelation and initiation.

Webre's hypothesis of this greater reality mirrors a powerful intuition, now shared by half of humanity, that we are not alone in the Universe. Many of those, in turn, believe that we are being visited and monitored to determine whether we should be permitted to emerge from the intergalactic quarantine. But these efforts are obviously being resisted by the plutocracy of vested interests in perpetual warfare and unsustainable resource exploitation – interests that suppress our transcendent truth for the sake of consolidating their own greed and power.

Much of this book rings true. Certainly, our civilization cannot go on as we have. We will need all the help we can get to lift ourselves out of tyranny, genocide, and ecocide. So why not reach out toward those who are clearly more wise?

Undoubtedly, more empirical evidence is needed to bolster the case for the ET presence and intention. Some of this is to be found in the excellent research of the late Dr. John Mack at Harvard. The contactees that Dr. Mack worked with have repeatedly reported the great sense of urgency that some off-planet cultures feel towards reversing humanity's destruction of Earth's environment.

In this work, intuition plus admittedly incomplete science combine to form a very compelling case for understanding why we may have been exposed to the UFO/ET phenomenon, yet at the same time are so cut off from and confused about the extraterrestrial realities that underlie the evidence.

About the Author

ALFRED LAMBREMONT WEBRE was a futurist at The Center for the Study of Social Policy at Stanford Research Institute (today, SRI International, Menlo Park, California). In that capacity, he served as Principal Investigator for a proposed civilian scientific study of extraterrestrial communication, i.e., interactive communication between our terrestrial human culture and that of possible intelligent Off-Planet Cultures. This proposed study was presented to and developed with interested members of the domestic policy staff of the White House of President Jimmy Carter, from the Spring of 1977 until the Fall of 1977, when it was abruptly terminated.

A Fulbright Scholar, Webre is a graduate of Yale University. He earned his Juris Doctor from Yale Law School, where he was a National Scholar, and completed the University of Texas Counseling Program. In addition to serving as a futurist at SRI, he was General Counsel to New York City's EPA and was an environmental consultant to the Ford Foundation. He has taught Economics at Yale and Civil Liberties at the University of Texas and is an author. He is a member of the District of Columbia Bar.

Webre was a delegate to the UNISPACE Outer Space Conference and an NGO representative at the United Nations (Communications Coordination Committee for the UN; UN Second Special Session on Disarmament); was elected a Clinton-Gore delegate to the 1996 Texas Democratic Convention; and served as a member of the Governor's Emergency Taskforce on Earthquake Preparedness for the State of California (1980-82), a position he was appointed to by Governor Jerry Brown. He produced and hosted The Instant of Cooperation, the first live radio broadcast between the United States and the former Soviet Union, which was carried live by Gosteleradio and NPR satellite radio in 1987.

Today, Webre is a space activist who works with others to prevent the weaponization of space and to transform the permanent war economy into a sustainable, peaceful, cooperative Space Age society reintegrated with a larger, intelligent Universe society. He is the International Director of the Institute for Cooperation in Space (ICIS); is a founder of the No Weapons in Space Campaign (NOWIS), a Canadian coalition to prevent the weaponization of space; and coordinates the Campaign for Cooperation in Space. He is an On-Air Host on Vancouver Coop Radio CFRO 102.7 FM, available at www.coopradio.org, and is the founder of Exopolitics.com: Politics, Government, and Law in the Universe, an Internet resource for Exopolitical discourse and advocacy.

Webre lives with his spouse, psychotherapist and psychic Geri DeStefano-Webre, Ph.D., in Vancouver, British Columbia.

Foreword by
Courtney Brown, Ph.D.

Associate Professor, Political Science, Emory University; Founder, The Farsight Institute (non-profit research and educational organization dedicated to the study of the "remote viewing" phenomenon)

AS RECENTLY AS THE first half of the 1990s, the dominant sense among most of the scientific community, as reported in the mainstream media, was that it is highly improbable that many other planets exist orbiting stars other than our own Sun. That is, many intelligent scientists held firmly to the view that Earth is a galactic anomaly. Planets orbiting other suns were assumed to be a rarity, and so Earth-type planets orbiting other suns were deemed to be exceptionally rare. This, of course, was a prelude to the belief that life in places other than Earth was doubtful in the extreme. The unspoken fear among these same scientists was that we might not really be alone in this Universe, and indeed, there may not be that much special about us at all.

From a scientific perspective, the proposition that the phenomenon of planets orbiting other suns would be a rare event has always been ludicrous. We live in a solar system with at least nine known major planets, a full-size asteroid belt, a host of comets, zillions of meteors, and enormous quantities of dust, all of which orbit our Sun. Moreover, most of the planets in our solar system have their own systems of moons. The only reasonable rule to draw from our own experience with our solar system is that nature seems to favour many bodies orbiting other bodies. Statistically, we have a sample of one (that is, one solar system) about which we know a great deal. Scientifically, we have no recourse but to establish our sample of one as the expected mean (that is, arithmetic average) for all solar systems – until additional data can be obtained and averaged, thereby allowing us to modify our estimate of this mean. We must also assume that there will be a distribution around this mean, which requires that some solar systems will have more planets, and other solar systems will have fewer planets. More specifically, there will be an expected mean or average number of planets orbiting each star, and the distribution of such planets orbiting their stars must have a standard deviation. This is a most basic application of statistics, and all scientists are wedded to the underlying mathematical assumptions of such things. To assume that our solar system is unique in our galaxy is to claim that our sample of one is an outlier, an anomaly. It is impossible to make this claim without a prior knowledge of the distribution of planets around other solar systems, since the idea of an outlier only makes sense in the context of a distribution. To insist, nonetheless, that our solar system is unique in the Universe thus violates a widely accepted approach to scientific thinking. Viewed in this light, the claim of uniqueness is an extreme position.

Let us now consider the obvious fact that our own solar system was created out of the same collection of cosmic dust from which all other solar systems were created in our area of the galaxy. It is doubtful that one would find much difference in the chemical makeup of our solar system in direct comparison with other solar systems within, say, a 100-light year radius. Since we all came out of the same cosmic soup, it is likely that there are many nearby solar systems in which planets exist which support conditions favourable to the initiation of life. Going back to statistics, we have a sample of one planet (that is, our Earth) in which life is phenomenally abundant and possesses tremendous variety. Life exists in all sorts of environmental extremes on this planet. Moreover, we finally have clear and unambiguous evidence that Mars also was once a warm and wet world, and scientists now confidently claim that meteors originating from Mars contain fossil evidence of Martian microbial life. Thus, we have a sample of one solar system in which life either exists or has existed on two planets. This must be our initial guess of the assumed expected mean for other solar systems, at least with respect to those solar systems residing within our neck of the galactic woods. There really is no alternative interpretation presently available to science, at least not in the absence of additional information suggesting something to the contrary.

Now we must turn to the topic of intelligent life. Intelligence is merely a matter of degree. If life has enough time in its evolutionary calendar, it is virtually certain that eventually one species on each life-supporting world will evolve in the direction of a larger and more capable brain. This will increase that species' ability to compete with less intelligent animals for food and survival. As is suggested by Edward O. Wilson's theories on the evolution of intelligence, bigger and more capable brains constitute a physiological trait comparable to other evolving physiological traits, and there is no evolutionary law prohibiting the development of any particular trait. From my perspective, the only reasonable and scientifically defensible conclusion that can be drawn from all of the above is that warm and wet Earth-type planets must be abundant, at least in our galaxy (although probably beyond it as well), and that life must be common. Moreover, given that time is the primary ingredient necessary for the evolution of intelligence, it seems most likely that intelligent life surrounds us as well.

Where is the evidence of such life? Just 10 years ago most mainstream scientists were asking the same type of question about the existence of planets orbiting other suns. Recent astronomical discoveries indicate that planets are much more common than was once thought, and scientists are just now considering the proposition that planets may indeed be ubiquitous. Similarly, I must argue that time will tell with respect to the matter of life on other worlds. It seems clear to me that the evidence of such life will eventually be found without ambiguity. Indeed, many would suggest (as I have done elsewhere) that ambiguity in regard to this matter is of our own making, that extraterrestrial life has already discovered us, and that our own governmental and corporate interests have prevented the masses from recognizing the obvious. Until this is resolved, doubting scientists still need to wrestle with the contradiction implied by their "convenient" dismissal of basic extrapolations of statistical theory. From a statistical perspective, to claim that a sample of one is an initial estimate of a mean is not extreme. To claim with fervent certainty that the sample of one is an outlier is both extreme and (at least in my mind) scientifically untenable. If such scientists argue that life on Earth is unique, then they must offer a compelling reason as to why we should not assume that life in our solar system is a sample of one, and that our first approximation of the average probability of life in other realms should not be drawn from the known traits of our own solar system.

Following a similar logic, it seems clear to me that intelligent life is a widespread reality in our galaxy, and we should begin to address the political as well as the scientific implications of this. Again, viewing our own planet as a sample of one, we have many cultures residing on Earth. Organizations have naturally formed on this planet, both as a means of defense from hostile neighbors and as a way to foster economic growth. As our planetary civilization has grown, the general trend over the thousands of years seems to be in the direction of avoiding war and building economies, although there do seem to have been some notable short-term exceptions to this more general historical trend. Thus, my suggestion is that we treat our own experience again as a sample of one. Where there is intelligent life in our galaxy, this life will most certainly tend to self-organize. Following this thought, we are not then merely surrounded by intelligent life, but by intelligent life that is organized into various groupings. Indeed, if our own planetary civilization can come up with the idea of a United Nations, I am certain that extraterrestrial civilizations would have no difficulty finding use for (and then developing) their own interplanetary versions of such an organization. I see no escape from the likelihood that there is some type of organization that exists among our nearby worlds that might as well be called a "Galactic Federation."

It is probable that there are natural limits to the size of political organizations of extraterrestrial worlds. That is, if there are, say, 60,000 planets in our galaxy that sustain intelligent life at any given time, then it is unlikely that all 60,000 would find the need to participate in a so-called "Galactic Federation." Indeed, I would think it much more likely that much smaller organizations would form which would serve the needs of their member societies with a greater eye toward "local service." Thus, an organization that would effectively serve our region of our galaxy may have only a few hundred members. More than that might prove unwieldy. Should there be a need to defend the interests of one member of such an organization from, say, the interloping activities of an outside group, it seems hardly conceivable that the resources of the entire galaxy would be required to defend those interests. A more manageable number of participants in such an organization would more likely be ideal – not so many as to be lost in the deck, but enough to offer a measure of collective security.

This brings me to the topic of Alfred Webre's new book on the topic of Exopolitics. Webre's perspective of how we should approach the issue of human interactions with organized extraterrestrial life is one that needs to be considered among the various alternative approaches. Thus, this book really is essential reading for anyone interested in the subject of intelligent extraterrestrial life. It seems to me obvious that as soon as one realizes that intelligent extraterrestrial life exists, the very next question is not a scientific one, but a political one. Moreover, one question leads inevitably to another. How does one interact with this life? How is it organized? Does it belong to an extraterrestrial organization? Do such organizations form for the purpose of planetary defense, or is there an alternate rationale for their existence? Are there interloping groups or societies about which there are elements of concern? Do extraterrestrial societies interact competitively, cooperatively, or both? What are the goals that drive such societies? Since it is reasonable to assume that interplanetary societies would have no difficulty finding natural resources such as water and minerals among any number of uninhabited worlds, what currency would such societies find valuable? Would genetic materials governing the variety of life be of ultimate value to such extraterrestrial civilizations? These are the sorts of questions that we simply cannot avoid any longer. Webre bravely inserts himself into this debate in its most formative stage of development. We all need to consider what he has to say.

Some may claim that Alfred Webre's views are utopian. This may or may not be true, and we will never know until we probe further into such issues. Meanwhile, Webre's views are without doubt a valid "first take" on the overall issue of how humans should interact with intelligent extraterrestrial life. Noting Webre's background, it may at first seem odd that the matter of extraterrestrial intelligence should be so quickly engaged by a person trained in matters of law. But this is the nature of self-organizing intelligence. Organizations survive because they embrace rules governing individual and collective behavior. Lawyers are trained to first understand those rules and then operationalize them. Science will help us to recognize that intelligent life other than our own exists in this Universe. After that, the lawyers and politicians will take over. Webre sees this far in advance of most others, and he wants to set the tone for the future political debates that are as inevitable as they will be profound. This is a book that we all need to have read before these debates become widespread in our society, before we are gripped by a fear of the new and the unknown that seems so readily to spring from within us. I suspect that fear will play no useful role in our future interactions with the extraterrestrials. We need to abandon fear.

Right now, if we could only get our species to look up with wonder at the potential vastness of life and its inherent complexity, we would be on a much better track than our current embrace of denial offers us. Webre's book is a hopeful and inspiring outlook concerning our future as a species. This is an outlook worth exploring in its fullness.

Foreword by
Paul Davids

Executive Producer and Co-Writer, *Roswell,* starring Kyle MacLachlan, Martin Sheen, and Dwight Yoakam (nominated for Golden Globe Award, Best Television Motion Picture, 1994)

TIME MAGAZINE HAS AN annual practice of selecting The Man (or Woman) of the Year. A more appropriate ritual for the new millennium might be to select The Mind of the Year, and if that were so, Alfred Lambremont Webre would rank high on my list of suggested nominees. Among modern philosophers, Webre finds himself one of a very select few at the center of the birth of a discipline of critical importance for the future – Exopolitics.

Exopolitics is the name of a new field of knowledge, research, philosophy, and imagination. Its purpose is to explore the relationship of humanity – past, present, and future – to other intelligent species originating from elsewhere in the Universe, including beings that may exist in other dimensions of time-space. Exopolitics shares a common inspiration with Exobiology (the study of extraterrestrial life forms) and Exoarcheology (the study of what might prove to be extraterrestrial structures and monuments on other celestial bodies). These disciplines are currently filled with much speculation, because the so-called "hard facts" are not yet transparent. One thing is certain, however, and that is that we are living at the beginning of an upheaval in modern thought as momentous as the Darwinian, Freudian, Einsteinian, and Watson-Crickian scientific leaps of thought that shaped the last century. The theories that underpin evolution, psychoanalysis, relativity, and DNA all suffered a difficult birth. So shall it be with Exopolitics.

Just as was the case with each of these other cornerstones of modern thought, the world has not yet woken up to the fact that the intellectual ground is about to shift under our feet all over again. In the case of Exopolitics, what lies ahead will be a cataclysm of momentous concepts that will move "Heaven and Earth" – or at least re-structure our thinking about humanity's place in the scheme of things. By this I mean much more than that our physical place in the Universe will be redefined. Exopolitics expands the biological scale upwards from where it now ends, with human beings at the pinnacle. For centuries, man has declared himself King of the Universe. Webre is a leader among those heralding the unpopular news that the King of the Universe is about to lose his crown. So swiftly will we be deposed, and such a blow will it be to the human ego, that there will be, in many quarters, a reactionary rejection of Webre's central idea. That rejection is likely to continue for as long as humanly possible and not a moment less. Paul Revere once said, "One if by land, two if by sea." Alfred Webre declares, "One if by land, two if by sea, three if from outer space!" The British establishment had nothing good to say about Paul Revere in the days of the American Revolution. And the establishment of the so-called civilized world today will probably have few niceties for the author of this book, at least for the moment. As in past eras of history, there will surely be a widespread desire to punish the messenger because of disdain for his message.

But what is the message? It is an affirmation of what science, politics and government have done their utmost to deny – that the Universe is vastly populated, throughout, by advanced biological species that are so far beyond us, that in many cases we are mere children by comparison. Arthur C. Clarke sounded the same message in his landmark work of science fiction, *Childhood's End*. In that book, the arrival of other species from distant regions of space marked the end of the intellectual childhood of the human race, and the beginning of our first glimpse of biological reality on a universal scale.

The book that you now hold in your hands purports to be something quite different from science fiction: a fairly precise outline of facts you may never have considered before. It is a "treatise." So was Sigmund Freud's *An Outline of Psychoanalysis*. Both share the trait that they are, more or less, the same length. They also share the characteristic that they are cornerstones of new thought. Brevity can move mountains when it strikes its target like an arrow piercing the bulls-eye, and Webre, like Freud, fully intends to move mountains, for the spirit of his treatise is, Upon this Rock shall the Future of Humankind be Built!

President Reagan once stood before the United Nations General Assembly and wondered aloud about what the effect would be if the human race were threatened by some alien civilization from "out there." For Webre, however, the issue is not one of a threat. It is an issue of the true nature of the relationship between interplanetary species. On a universal scale, he sets forth purported interactions of beings from multiple worlds that are tantamount to a sort of intergalactic diplomacy. That diplomacy, as in Webre's title, includes politics, government and law, but on a universal scale. By contrast, the politics, government and laws of Earth are seen as mere holograms of larger realities and cosmic principles.

I was asked to write this foreword because I was principally involved in the Showtime original motion picture *Roswell*, a film that challenged the old order of thinking that still claims that no contact with ET intelligence has yet occurred. This film raised the specter of government secrecy and the desire of authorities to refrain from revealing the facts about intelligent extraterrestrial life forms to the public. *Roswell* opened the floodgates on these issues. It presented a rather relentless case that highly placed officials and powerful institutions within the United States government have secreted the hard-core, open-and-shut evidence of advanced extraterrestrial life since at least 1947. It dramatized the notion that the art of lying about what is secretly and officially known about visitors from outer space has become an institutionalized and ironclad policy.

Roswell explores the theme that not only has there been a never-ending policy of deceit and denial, but there has been an effort to trivialize this subject of paramount importance and to stigmatize those who take it seriously. Efforts have been made to relegate flying saucers, aliens, and space visitors who arrived on our planet in ancient times to the realm of "fringe" subjects, the domain of eccentrics and kooks. And why would such a policy have been implemented? Jack Nicholson said it best in another film, *A Few Good Men*, when he declared, "Because you can't handle the truth!" But the truth would not have been concealed with such effort merely to save the majority of us psychotherapy bills. There would have been many other advantages to withholding the facts of extraterrestrial contact. These included issues of political control and economic power.

A decade following the first broadcast of our movie, I can't swear on a stack of Bibles that its premise is fact. I wasn't there when the Roswell event happened. However, to accept the official view – that nothing of consequence happened at Roswell – one has to disregard the sworn testimony of dozens of military men and civilians who were in Roswell at the time, and whose affidavits and testimonials are all on public display at the International UFO Museum and Research Center in Roswell, New Mexico.

Hollywood and science fiction novelists have long had the intriguing new field of Exopolitics all to themselves. Think back to 1950, and *The Day The Earth Stood Still*, when Klaatu, the name of the alien played by Michael Rennie, stood on the rim of his flying saucer before the throngs of Washington, DC and gave a blunt ultimatum to the human race. To paraphrase his message of admonition, he said, "Abandon your war-faring ways, for if you fail to do so, if you attempt to take your weapons into space and thereby threaten other civilizations in the Universe, you will be destroyed by powers that you cannot even imagine. The choice is yours." That was one of the cinema's first dramatizations of Exopolitics.

In *The War of the Worlds*, which was one of four seminal motion pictures producer George Pal contributed to the realm of Exopolitics, based on the novel by H. G. Wells, the human race had not even a choice about its ultimate fate. The choice had already been made by land-grabbing Martians to annihilate us. The same occurred once again in Independence Day, but they weren't from Mars. In Gene Roddenberry's *Star Trek*, the universal Exopolitics proved complex precisely because the Universe was populated with so many species that had different agendas and goals. In George Lucas's *Star Wars*, we learned that the Exopolitics of interplanetary relations began "A long time ago, in a galaxy far, far away," and that those relations were none too friendly. In films such as *Cocoon* and Steven Spielberg's *Close Encounters of the Third Kind*, the aliens came for a select few of us, and those few seemed to be promised a life of harmony "up there." In *Fire in the Sky*, the aliens who abducted Travis Walton seemed to have less angelic plans for his experience in space, and they soon spewed him out, putting him back on terra firma as naked as the day he was born. In *Forbidden Planet*, the Exopolitics of time and space came under the control of one scientist, Dr. Morbius, who while stranded on the planet Altair 4, mastered the advanced, secret technologies of a long-extinct alien race, the Krell, which he offered to dole out in small bits and pieces to Earth only when he, in his "infinite wisdom," saw fit to do so.

So, to paraphrase the classic song, what's it all about, Alfred? I think it's appropriate to pose that question to the author, because Alfred Lambremont Webre is one of the few who may have now actually answered the question, and in the very work that follows. His answer goes something like this: We sometimes call ourselves "The Children of God." Indeed, even when we are elderly we are still essentially like children, newborns in an ancient Universe, in which biological intelligence has developed many times, in many places across the vastness of space, a Universe in which one species has begotten others, using the tools of genetic engineering, again and again, throughout the eons of time.

In the Universe according to Webre, most of the other neighbors in the Universe know one another. They have formed what Webre calls "Universe Society." They also know us, the people of Earth. One problem has been that we do not know them. Another problem has been that they have placed us under quarantine. We are contained, like the lepers of Molokai in a previous century. But the duration of our quarantine may be coming to a close, and that will create both great opportunities and cause powerful shock waves for humanity. A third problem has been that a long line of American Presidents, as well as the New York Times, TIME, news anchors from Walter Cronkite to Tom Brokaw, Senators and Congressmen, university science professors, directors of NASA, and other authoritative voices about Who's Who and What's What, have all denied that there is any proof that intelligent extraterrestrial species exist and that they have visited Earth. They have chosen instead to open the door just a crack, by offering fossil evidence of ancient bacteria-like life forms from Mars, found in an ancient meteorite, and even that evidence is hotly disputed.

For those of us who have dealt with this problem in earnest, who have read every claim about alien-human contact, who have collected every testimonial of the several astronauts and the few other people of renown who have "talked," the evidence for advanced extraterrestrial life appears to be quite overwhelming. We can see that the problem has been that the lords and the ladies of establishment opinion have somehow managed to create an impenetrable veil of illusion, in which neither they nor the public can see the evidence that is right in front of our faces, nor even discuss extraterrestrial life without smirks and ridicule. If the emperor has no clothes, they are certainly not admitting it. Fortunately, there are a few exceptions. Check out the provocative appendix of this book for the views of certain opinion leaders who do indeed believe that ET has not only phoned home, he has visited ours!

In the end, hopefully the truth will win out, for its arc is as long as the Universe is incomprehensibly vast. Pivotal works, such as Alfred Webre's *Exopolitics*, may play an important role in preparing many minds to comprehend that down here on the Planet Earth, the handwriting – of the aliens – is on the wall.

Caveat Lector

Our human civilization is at the very beginning of its era of universal consciousness. Any factual errors in descriptions of the structure of a Universe government and of the dynamics of Universe politics, although they may be intuitively well-founded, are the sole responsibility of the author.

PART ONE

Turning the Universe Upside Down

HOW MOST OF THE story modern human beings have been told about Earth and its outer space environs is wrong. How it is logical and rational that we live in a highly populous and organized Universe society of life-bearing planets. How Universe politics has placed Earth in a planetary quarantine. How that quarantine may be lifting, and what we can do to hasten a universal reunion.

1

Introduction to Exopolitics

The Exopolitics Model

IS THERE INTELLIGENT LIFE elsewhere in the Universe? Exopolitics, as a discipline for understanding Universe society through its politics and government, may turn our dominant view of the Universe upside down. Exopolitics posits that the truest conception of our earthly circumstance may be that we are on an isolated planet in the midst of a populated, evolving, highly organized inter-planetary, inter-galactic, multi-dimensional Universe society.

Exopolitics provides us with a 21st century universal paradigm, a new dominant world-view. The scientific paradigm of the 20th century was that intelligent life ended at Earth's geo-stationary orbit. The Exopolitics model informs us that, in reality, Earth appears to be an isolated planet in the midst of a populated Universe. Universe society consists of advanced, highly organized, and consciously evolving civilizations. Universe civilizations function within our own interstellar Universe, as well as within other dimensions in the Universe-at-large. Advanced Universe civilizations exist in other dimensions parallel to our own. They access not only our own planet and galaxy but also all of interstellar space.

In the Exopolitics model, life-bearing planets such as Earth are members of a collective Universe whole that operates under universal law. Think of Earth as part of a universal commons. Life was planted and cultivated here under the stewardship of more advanced societies, in accordance with the over-all principles of Universe ecology.

Our Exopolitics model holds that, when necessary, universal law applies restrictive measures to a planet when it endangers the collective whole.

Universe government can remove a planet from open circulation within Universe society. This fate appears to have happened to Earth in our distant past. Earth has suffered for eons as an exopolitical outcast among the community of Universe civilizations.

The Exopolitics model holds that Earth is presently isolated from interaction with organized intergalactic civilization because it is under intentional quarantine by a rational, structured Universe society. There are signs around us, however, of a Universe initiative to reintegrate Earth into interplanetary society. It is possible that Earth may be permitted to rejoin Universe society, under certain conditions, at a future time certain.

The Exopolitics Model and Public Opinion

This interpretation of our universal reality may seem vaguely familiar to you. It is, after all, the stock-in-trade of most science fiction. The notion of a populated Universe may have the ring of truth to you. It may raise a tingle on the back of your neck, or be a truth too close for comfort. You may even react to the concept of a populated Universe as flaky and unscientific.

Are humanity and our planet on the verge of being re-integrated into Universe society? That's very likely. The signs are all around us. In-depth public opinion polls evidencing positive contemporary human attitudes about a Universe populated with intelligent civilizations are important signs of our pending re-integration into Universe society.

The Exopolitics model is an operational bridge between our terrestrial politics, government, and law, and the larger models of politics, government, and law in Universe society. Exopolitics may be a key institutional nexus for navigating Earth's reintegration into Universe society. Exopolitics is a political, governmental, and legal process by which the interests of human society – its individuals, institutions, and nations – can reach out to, interact with, and create a cooperative future with off-planet cultures (OPCs).

Exopolitics does not end at Earth's edge but is a process universal in its reach. Earth's reintegration into Universe society may be occurring as part of a definable exopolitical process within Universe society itself.

Your own beliefs about a populated Universe – whatever they might be – fall along a spectrum of public opinion that has been frequently measured. A Gallup poll in 1996, for example, showed that 72 percent of the US adult population believes there is some form of extraterrestrial life, and 45 percent believes the Earth has already been visited by extraterrestrial beings. There are indications that public opinion about extraterrestrial visitation is similar in other regions of the planet. The proportion of extraterrestrial-sensitive world youth may be even higher than that in the adult population that believes in an extraterrestrial presence.

Nearly 100 million US respondents (or 45 percent of the adult US population) believe that extraterrestrial civilizations have visited Earth. This is approximately the same number of citizens of the United States that votes in US Presidential elections. The US Federal Election Commission reported that 96,277,634 people voted in the 1996 presidential election, and about 100,000,000 persons voted in the disputed 2000 US Presidential election. It would seem that in the United States about as many individuals believe in extraterrestrial life as believe in voting for President!

It is safe to assume that the 100 million adult US respondents to the poll who said they believe in extraterrestrial life cannot all be deluded, programmed, or brainwashed. These extraterrestrial-sensitive humans are responding to something that they sense, deeply and intuitively, is true – extraterrestrials are visiting Earth, and this fact is being suppressed. It is also safe to assume that human intuition is reality-oriented enough to filter out the disinformation propagated to obscure universal reality. For example, some extraterrestrial "visitations" are actually psychological warfare operations conducted by military and intelligence agencies of decidedly human origin.

Other public opinion polls confirm the role of intuition in shaping belief about extraterrestrial life. An ABC-NEWS poll in October 2000 found that 47% of US adults believe that intelligent life exists on other planets in the Universe. Demographically, the poll found that belief in extraterrestrial life is held by more men (51%) than women (43%); more college-educated citizens (51%) than high school graduates (43%); more Democrats (53%) than Republicans (38%).

The ABC-NEWS poll found that 60 percent of those who think intelligent extraterrestrial life exists also believe that extraterrestrials have visited Earth. Overall, 27% of adult US respondents said they believe that extraterrestrials visit Earth. (Interestingly, the poll excluded "spiritual alien" and "telepathic alien" visits.)

As with the Gallup poll in 1996, personal intuition appears to be a key component of human opinion that intelligent extraterrestrial life exists and visits Earth. In the ABC-NEWS poll in 2000, fully two-thirds of those who responded that they think extraterrestrials visit Earth stated that they based their conclusion on "speculation." One-third of respondents base their opinion on external evidence they have read or seen. Intuition may therefore be the basis for the insights of at least two-thirds of extraterrestrial-sensitive persons.

Estimates of the percentage of the US population that thinks extraterrestrial civilizations visit Earth range from 45% in the Gallup poll in 1996 to 27% of the adult population in the ABC-NEWS poll in 2000. Somewhere between 50 million and 100 million adults in the United States alone believe beings from extraterrestrial civilizations visit Earth, and the United States comprises only five percent of the world's total population.

On November 11th, 1999, a less statistically based poll (one that included a number of leading astronomers and astrophysicists) was released in the United States in a documentary broadcast on cable television. Seventy percent of those surveyed said they believe there is intelligent life in the Universe, including our own Milky Way galaxy. Eighty percent said they believe alien civilizations are more advanced than Earth's. Sixty-five percent of the participants said they think Earth would be conquered if aliens chose to "invade" us. Twenty-six percent said they think that if the Earth is invaded, the people of Earth will fight back and win.

These polls may, in fact, indicate a bottom-line reality about the Universe that the poll participants intuitively sense: we humans are actually part of a highly advanced, organized, interstellar civilization, from which we are in deliberate isolation. This Universe society of intelligent, planetary civilizations is a highly organized and civilized interstellar government that would not attack Earth because it is not violent, war-like, or destructive. Although Earth is currently in isolation from the rest of interplanetary society, we are part of a peaceful Universe government.

The Quarantine Hypothesis
and the UFO Phenomenon

YOU MAY ASK, "WHAT is the evidence that an inter-dimensional, interplanetary Universe society exists, and is presently lifting its intentional quarantine of Earth?" We find a conclusive answer in recent scientific analysis of the evidence of high-quality Unidentified Flying Object (UFO) encounters.

The UFO Phenomenon

The UFO phenomenon began in full force around our planet in 1947. The quarantine hypothesis holds that UFOs are an integral part of humanity's reintegration into interplanetary society. Some UFO phenomena appear primarily to be deployed by a higher intelligence as psychological conditioning tools. In an ongoing analysis of the UFO phenomenon, psychologist Carl Jung stated in 1955, "A purely psychological explanation is ruled out [to explain UFOs]... [T]he discs show signs of intelligent guidance, by quasi-human pilots..." Jung concluded that UFOs function essentially as "Mandalas" or spiritual conditioning symbols meant to facilitate humanity's spiritual evolution.[1]

The UFO phenomenon operates as a key force in raising human awareness of Universe society, regardless of whether its specific source is terrestrial or extraterrestrial. Our Universal awareness is automatically increased by a UFO experience, whether created by a higher intelligent civilization, a natural phenomenon like electromagnetic pulse energy, or a military-intelligence disinformation program.

UFO or "alien abduction"experiences simulated by military and intelligence agencies, as a form of disinformation, may momentarily trick human subjects into thinking "bad" aliens are occupying Earth. At the same time, these disinformation-driven UFO encounters are propelling forward humanity's awareness of higher intelligence in the Universe.

Operationally, the UFO phenomenon appears to be a mix of all of the following:

1. *Dimensional Psychological Conditioners.* Some UFOs are electro-magnetically generated "virtual reality" images of spacecraft, as well as spiritual symbols (such as Mandalas). These are created by Universe society, advanced dimensional beings, or the collective human mind, to condition us into universal awareness that we are part of an interplanetary society. The "UFOs" function as peripheral cues to our collective consciousness.

2. *Interplanetary Spacecraft.* Other UFOs are actual interplanetary spacecraft that are part of an extraterrestrial initiative to integrate Universe society.

3. *Covert Military Craft.* Still other UFOs are Top Secret, black budget military-intelligence craft, which masquerade as extraterrestrial "spacecraft." These secret craft implement a covert disinformation scenario, including mind control-based "military abductions" (MILABs), in furtherance of "psy ops" – psychological warfare operations – purporting extraterrestrial "invasion" of Earth.

4. *Natural Phenomena.* UFOs are also caused by natural phenomena like electromagnetic pulse energy or clouds, which may be configured into the archetype of "spacecraft" and other archetypal symbols by an intelligent civilization or by the human collective unconscious.

The Extraterrestrial "Leaky Embargo" Strategy

A community of scientists has addressed how it is that advanced extraterrestrial civilizations may be in our environment, all around us, yet in a stealth mode, so that human society remains oblivious to their presence. Scientists like Dr. Hal Puthoff and his colleagues at the Institute for Advanced Studies in Austin conclude that "some evidence of [the extraterrestrial] presence might be found in certain high quality UFO reports… and that such advanced extraterrestrial civilizations may value the search for knowledge from uncontaminated species [like humans] more than direct, interspecies communication, thereby accounting for apparent covertness regarding their presence." [2]

Dr. Puthoff and his colleagues conclude that the existence of a planetary quarantine that he terms a "Leaky Embargo" can be verified by the evidence of high quality UFO encounters. The term "Leaky Embargo" refers to the fact that the UFO encounters that we experience on Earth are actually intentional "leaks" in what is otherwise a total quarantine of Earth by advanced extraterrestrial civilizations. The Leaky Embargo is, according to these scientists, a "grassroots education program" of humanity in the form of the UFO phenomenon that started around 1947.

Exopolitics and the Planetary Quarantine

We know from the naval blockade of Cuba by the United States during the Cuban Missile Crisis in 1962 and from the United Nations' embargo of Iraq during 1991 to 2003 that embargos require concerted social action by the parties carrying them out. Just imagine what it would require to carry out a quarantine of Earth in the midst of a populated Universe. The Exopolitics model holds that the Earth's quarantine is not a random event, but the product of an organized intelligent Universe society. The Leaky Embargo described by Dr. Puthoff and his colleagues is another way of saying that the planetary quarantine is lifting, and that the UFO phenomenon that started in 1947 is the beginning of the lifting of this quarantine.

One requirement of carrying out a quarantine of Earth is technical. How is the quarantine to be carried out? Another aspect of quarantine is legal. On whose authority is a quarantine of Earth first imposed and then enforced over time, and with the precision that one notes in high quality UFO encounters?

The context communication theory of extraterrestrial communication, developed in 1974, holds that interactions with extraterrestrial civilizations, such as UFO encounters, are actually purposeful communications by the extraterrestrial civilization. The content of these extraterrestrial communications can be interpreted contextually, through a process analogous to the principles that psychologists use to interpret dreams. According to the context communication theory, verified flights by UFOs over intercontinental ballistic missile bases and nuclear power facilities are warnings to humanity about the dangers of nuclear war. This "Leak" in the Leaky Embargo of Earth is likely a highly orchestrated part of a coordinated plan by extraterrestrial civilizations.

Technically, the quarantine of Earth is achieved by way of the superior technology and advanced evolution of Universe society. Universe government enforces an interplanetary and inter-dimensional quarantine of Earth by applying advanced principles in parascience: reflectivity and dimensionality, mediated through Universe governmental institutions, in the nature of a galactic federation of life-bearing planets.

Reflectivity uses the holistic energy of a being, a planet, or a constellation for deep understanding of, or communication with, that being, planet, constellation, and so forth. In present-day Earth terms, the principle of reflectivity comes into play when a psychic healer attunes to the aura or energy field surrounding a patient, and obtains a holistic picture of the patient's being. In human health care, this branch of science is known as "energy medicine."

Dimensionality is based on the dimensional structure and function of the Universe, and utilizes the multi-dimensions of the Universe for everything from advanced space travel to intelligent, spiritual "soul" evolution. Even in conventional Earth science, dimensionality is supported by recent human scientific advances, which now predict the demise of "time" and "space" in favour of a multi-dimensional reality.

Advanced Universe civilizations can gauge and monitor the relative "holistic state" of human society and Planet Earth. Through technologies and intelligence based on the principles of reflectivity and dimensionality, interplanetary civilization can monitor humans on Earth. If we think no one is watching Earth, we are in error. Universe government appears to be continually monitoring Earth, and has been monitoring our planet and our species since their inception.

This monitoring is positive and caring, like a gardener with a greenhouse or an ethical scientist with a cherished biological investigation. Earth is a life-experiment planet, and most of the life forms on Earth have been seeded and carefully cultivated by Universe society scientists. These Universe scientists are advanced beings that specialize in the growing and cultivation of planets. Reflectivity is one principle and technology by which they monitor the ups and downs of the planet and, where necessary, both individuals and groups of human beings.

The quarantine hypothesis supports dimensional interstellar travel as a reality of interplanetary society. Interstellar travel to and from Earth uses the inner dimensions of the Universe. This way, visitors to, and permanent observers of, Earth do not have to traverse the full distance of interstellar space. What we know as outer space is only one of reality's dimensions in the time-space continuum and beyond. Dimensionality is probably one of the most useful technologies that advanced societies can offer to humanity.

In the quarantine hypothesis, Earth's humanity is not yet sufficiently morally evolved to be unilaterally included in a Universe "dimensional" role. Universe society does not want us to export war or violence into interstellar or inter-dimensional space. The powerful nations of Earth, led by a secret command-and-control network in the United States, are attempting to continue the militarization of outer space. These Earth nations are on a collision course with Universe society's ethics and laws pertaining to the peaceful use of space. The militarization of outer space may be the single most important factor preventing the end of Earth's isolation from civilized space society. Humanity may not be permitted into Universe society without an absolute ban on warfare and weapons in a jurisdiction ruled by the standards of a common Universe government.

3

The Planetary
Quarantine and Its Causes

THE QUARANTINE SCENARIO IS a working model of our actual planetary history and present Universal reality. The quarantine from Universe society affects our entire reality – physical, social, emotional, mental, and spiritual. As a consequence, we have evolved under conditions that are the opposite for a normal life-bearing planet. In light of these factors, let's take a closer look at the quarantine and its causes.

Although a new sun is created in our galaxy every day, life-bearing planets like Earth do not appear willy-nilly in the slow evolutionary cycles of the Universe. Life-bearing planets are intentional experiments of advanced Universe society. Designated Universe scientists routinely monitor planets deemed capable of bearing life. When a planet like Earth appears to have favourable life-bearing conditions, Universe society formally incorporates the planet into a life creation program. Then, a slow, patient, intelligent life implantation program begins.

Planetary life implantation programs are not solely biological. Where planetary conditions are appropriate, life implantation processes can produce intelligent species like humans that are both biological and spiritual. Advanced species like us have both biological and spiritual components – body, mind, soul, and spirit.

Planets are grown like gardens. Much of life development on Planet Earth is the product of conscious intervention by the advanced, sophisticated techniques of the life-technologists of Universe society. This process takes billions of years. As our human scientists uncover more of the scientific past of our planet, they are actually discovering the work products of highly advanced agents within our Universe.

At a certain point in planetary evolution, intelligent life comes into being as part of the life experimentation scheme. With this intelligent life comes the human soul, a trans-temporal entity that experiences life as a human, and survives bodily death into other dimensions of the Universe. A new life implantation phase accompanies the appearance of intelligent souls on a planet. The planet is placed on a different life experiment track. Intelligent soul-creatures have evolved that can themselves eventually help to further creation in the Universe.

The quarantine hypothesis holds that soul-bearing planets are visited and developed by formal planetary representatives of Universe society. These Universe representatives are charged with "civilizing" the planet into Universe citizenship. Universe representatives are formally delegated to the life-bearing planet to oversee and guide its entrance into organized interplanetary society. On normal life experiment planets, general knowledge of, and participation in, interplanetary society occurs from the outset of civilization. On non-quarantined planets, an aspect of being civilized means consciously being part of interplanetary society. The quarantine hypothesis suggests that Earth did not integrate into Universe society in the normal way.

Causes of Earth's Quarantine

Exopolitics is the discipline that will lead us to new discoveries about our societal place in the Universe, including our societal past. At present, we do not know for certain what the historical reasons are for the quarantine of Earth. These answers may come as we integrate with Universe society and discover the facts that lie behind our isolation. It may be that we are embargoed, as Dr. Hal Puthoff holds, because we are still in a relatively primitive state of civilization, and are being fed hints on a piecemeal basis that extraterrestrial civilizations exist.

Exopolitical integration with off-planet cultures may confirm a different, and in some ways, more familiar interpretation of our planetary isolation, one which has resonance in human religious tradition and mythology. The sacred texts of our great religions may contain fragmentary myths in allegorical format that are based on an historical truth that Earth has been in intentional quarantine. This quarantine has isolated our planet (and our solar system) from communication with organized interplanetary society.

One such sacred text is the Book of Genesis with its allegory of the expulsion of the first two humans from the Garden of Eden. At least one purported exopolitical source text, *The Urantia Book*, holds that the Book of Genesis refers in mythical form to actual events in the exopolitical history of Earth. By this account, the Book of Genesis is a fragmentary, allegorical version of an early exopolitical colonization of Earth that resulted in catastrophic failure and the subsequent expulsion or quarantine of Earth from the network of inhabited planets under the jurisdiction of the Universe government.[3]

As a form of evidentiary cross-check, another set of exopolitical data, developed by scientific remote viewing [a scientific protocol for interacting telepathically with intelligent entities outside of a specific framework of time and space][4], confirms that *The Urantia Book*'s exopolitical source text is generally accurate in its depiction of the Adam and Eve story and its catastrophic relation to Earth's exopolitical history as the cause of Earth's Universe quarantine. The scientist developing this data notes: "Nonetheless, because *The Urantia Book*'s discussion of Adam and Eve has a distinct ET flavour, I decided to have my monitor add this famous pair to my [scientific remote viewing] target list... But as it turned out, the story of Adam and Eve in *The Urantia Book* is basically accurate... Some readers may wonder why the religious figures of Adam and Eve would be a target of investigations in a book about extraterrestrials. The basic reason... is that many of our human myths may have some basis in history."[5]

We do not now know to an absolute certainty the detailed facts of this catastrophic planetary rebellion or other key events in Earth's exopolitical past. We can uncover our exopolitical history by open social integration with spiritually advanced extraterrestrial civilizations now visiting Earth. Whatever the actual details of the catastrophic rebellion against the Universe administration, the purpose of the quarantine of Earth was to prevent the exopolitical rebellion that occurred in our solar system from spreading out into the Universe. The quarantine has allowed the effects of this exopolitical rebellion on Earth to take their natural course and eventually to heal. The UFO encounters of the Leaky Embargo provide current evidence that Earth is now entering a period of re-integration with organized Universe society.

We humans are the children of a universal cataclysmic event suffered in the course of our planetary evolution. Our subsequent planetary isolation accounts for the severely conflicted, violent, ignorant, and confused state of our history and our society. It is no accident that humans are cursed with war, violence, poverty, ignorance, and death. The violence of the 20th century would not have occurred on a normal life-bearing planet that had not experienced such an evolutionary disaster.

One aspect of the quarantine is that Earth's Universe circuits of communication and advanced energy have been cut off, throwing our planet into devolution. Earth was isolated from the rest of interplanetary society, and placed in quarantine. As a result of the quarantine, Earth has been historically deprived of normal planetary evolution and education. We have been kept in the dark about Universe society, and the advanced technologies and superior quality of life that normal planets enjoy.

In our individual lives and collective culture, humans have had to face more ignorance than a comparable intelligent civilization would confront on another planet. Our planetary quarantine allows the full effects of the planetary cataclysm to play out.

The flip side of Earth's enforced isolation is that we humans have emerged as a hardy species of intelligent spiritual entities, or souls. At their core, life-bearing planets are designed as laboratories for growing souls. The Universe is ultimately a spiritual domain, and a key goal of developing life-bearing planets is to provide developmental opportunities for growing souls (the non-temporal components of created beings).

With the isolation of Earth from hands-on guidance by Universe representatives, this planet has become a brief and intense testing ground for new and old souls alike. Apparently, Earth has quite a reputation in the Universe as a challenging but rewarding place to live through a human life. Future exopolitical research, perhaps with the officials, historians, and archives of Universe society itself, promises to be one avenue for discovering more facts, information, and truths about our exopolitical past.

4

A Universal Career

ONE LONG-TERM BENEFIT arising from Earth's quarantine is that our isolation has helped build a soul that can live on hope alone. Our human souls must reach deep into inner resources to overcome many of the lingering tendencies of the planetary quarantine, such as war, confusion, poverty, violence, and ignorance.

From the viewpoint of a Universe career, Earth's challenges may be ideal circumstances during the course of our lengthy evolution. A Universe career spans much longer than a single human lifetime on Planet Earth. Human souls progress on a path of development in a multi-dimensional Universe, with individual outcomes dependent upon our choices and actions in our Universe lives.

Looking at your life, fearlessly, as a universal adventure deepens its meaning. Planning your life is more than a cradle-to-grave exercise. A successful life career includes activities and in-depth orientations that endow the soul for its continued career in subsequent lifetimes. Life on Earth is part of one continuous cycle for the human soul that extends into other, non-temporal dimensions.

Religion has always spoken of the eternal existence of the human soul. A Universe career, however, is certainly not part of the modern scientific canon. Conventional science holds that all life ends at death, a concept that parascience, the new science, now disputes. Because of our disrupted, quarantined past on Earth, human awareness of the universal career as a dimension of life lay truncated and buried.

Modern materialism is but a developmental stage of a lower intelligent species as it evolves into a higher-order intelligent species. An advanced planetary society has it all. More advanced planets have a high level of civilization and standard of living, along with the knowledge that a material life is but a transitory stage of development for a more fundamental, non-temporal being known as the soul.

There is no challenge greater for modern human beings, caught up in the materialistic daily chaos of Earth, than to acknowledge the soul as the inner core of their being. Our human body, persona, identity, and desires are but costumes that the soul uses in its inexorable development toward union with universal source. Advanced civilizations in interplanetary (and inter-dimensional) society know these soul lessons well, for the Universe is a spiritual realm, and its core tasks are spiritual.

PART TWO

Universe Politics

HOW HUMANITY IS ULTIMATELY governed by universal law, which operates much like other natural and governmental laws on Earth. How politics and government do not stop at Earth's edge. How our position in interplanetary society is determined by what human society as a whole does on Earth – all politics are local, global, and then universal. How a planetary security system based on militarization and war effectively cuts us off from universal affairs. How a progressive planetary society sets the stage for political reintegration into Universe society.

5

Universe Politics is
Like All Human Politics

EXOPOLITICS – LIKE HUMAN POLITICS – is a social food fight. In the case of Universe politics on Earth, however, the food fight is one-sided. As a politically captive population, we humans are officially oblivious to the governing process of Universe society. Unofficially, of course, between one-quarter and one-half of the human population intuits that Earth is in a dynamic relationship with extraterrestrial civilizations.

Innate awareness of a larger Universe society is part of our human makeup, our evolution as a species. Social forms in the Universe are but holographic reflections of the Universe as a whole. Governmental and political structures on Earth are reflections as well, holographic fragments of larger forms in Universe society.

One of the remarkable qualities of Universe government is that its patterns and structure are holographic projections of the whole. In a hologram, the whole of the holographic projection is contained in each part of the hologram. By analogy, the governmental structure of the Universe as a whole is contained and reflected in governmental and political structures of its constituent parts, like Planet Earth.

The legacy of Earth's planetary isolation and quarantine differs, however, from a planet the evolution of which has followed a more regular, overtly Universe path. Earth's governmental forms both reflect the quarantine period and are fundamental holographic fragments of the Universe ideal.

Earth is a life-experiment planet under the jurisdiction of Universe society. Earth's heritage as a life-experiment planet is the reason why both human intuition and our sacred religious traditions contain so many partial truths about universal reality. Earth's political forms have their holographic, essential origin in Exopolitics, the political forms of Universe society. Consequently, Universe society's governmental and political forms are deeply embedded in the design of Earth's governmental structures.

"As above, so below" is a fundamental axiom of exopolitical evolution. That Earth does not openly participate in Universe politics is ironic. Humans are uniquely adaptive when it comes to politics. Witness our survival, for example, in the political twists and turns of the 20th century, let alone the entire planetary quarantine. As we achieve critical mass in human universal awareness, it will seem like the human community has always intuitively known that we are part of a larger, structured whole.

The principles of Exopolitics are straightforward. The basics of Universe politics are easily understood, even when applied to a quarantined planet like Earth with an irregular political history.

We humans are much closer to Universe politics than our millennia of isolation from Universe society might suggest. After Universe scientists genetically seeded us and human beings and human society became evolutionary descendants of Universe society, the early concepts of government were established on Earth under the guidance of Universe colonizers.

Exopolitics – Universe politics – is a structured process by which the evolutionary and social needs of life-bearing planets are determined and mediated. There are at least two sides to Earth's extraterrestrial politics: the needs of Universe society and the needs of our unique, quarantined planet. Because humans are largely oblivious of our isolation in a highly governed Universe, Earth's Exopolitics are elementary and simplistic.

Earth's Exopolitics are those of an intelligent civilization that is only now becoming conscious of its potential role in the larger Universe. A growing Universe consciousness on Earth means that an exopolitical process is beginning to unfold here as well. Humanity is moving toward liberating itself from a quarantined isolation imposed from above. We are deconstructing the narrow social and institutional blinders that have kept us in isolation from interstellar society. You and I are witnessing the beginnings of a Universe "process of liberation" of Planet Earth.

6

Universe Politics Does Not Stop at Earth's Edge

AT THIS STAGE IN Earth's development, an open mind is the best Universe navigation tool. Politics and government do not stop at Earth's edge. Exopolitics pervades the Universe. Universe governance is based upon rational principles. Universe society extends throughout known interstellar dimensions, as well as to Universe dimensions that our civilization has yet to discover.

Universe governance is based on the fundamental principle that spiritual and material dimensions in the Universe are a single reality. Spiritual reality is actually more "real" than material reality. Advanced extraterrestrial civilizations are based on acknowledging the unity of spirit and matter. Universe governance is based on the principle that the spiritual and material aspects of planetary evolution are intertwined, and seeks common evolutionary goals.

Universe society extends throughout the entire Cosmos. Its basic unit of organization is the life-bearing planet. Universe society constantly monitors intelligent civilizations on life-bearing planets. At a certain stage in the evolution of a life-bearing planet, its intelligent civilization becomes part of Universe governance. This is how Earth's early civilization originally became part of Universe society.

Consider one very rough but useful analogy. As a member of Universe society, our planet may be comparable to a town or city within a state or province inside a nation here on Earth. Of course, there are huge differences in this analogy. Governmental jurisdictions on Earth do not necessarily follow the lines of nature. Many Earthly borders and boundaries between counties, provinces, states, or nations, for example, cut across the natural lines of rivers, mountain systems, and ecosystems. Likewise, governmental systems of planets do not necessarily follow the physical structure of interstellar space.

Life-bearing planets in interstellar space form part of a vast, dynamic, inter-dimensional federation, structured around organic quadrants of universal creation, and composed of vibrant, varied exopolitical networks. Interstellar society is generally built around locally contiguous networks of life-bearing planets. Local networks of planets are entry-level building blocks of a decentralized exopolitical structure. Universe society operates across multi-dimensional realities, and includes many different forms of Universe civilizations – both "spiritual" and "material."

Advanced multi-dimensional civilizations actively propagate the myriad galaxies, stars, and solar systems of the physical Universe. Responsibility for conscious evolution of the Universe is decentralized. Ancient, multi-dimensional civilizations consciously evolve the Universe through advanced, scientific interventions in natural evolutionary processes. These inter-dimensional, "spiritual" societies create and cultivate intelligent civilizations such as our own. In turn, humanity itself has the potential to evolve into an advanced, multi-dimensional society. The adage "Ye are Gods in the making" expresses this evolutionary truth.

Universe society plans and develops basic networks of life-experiment planets in contiguous quadrants of outer space. Life-experiment specialists develop these planetary networks over long eons of time. Life-bearing planets are formally incorporated into Universe governance networks as their intelligent civilizations mature. Once a single planetary network reaches the limits of manageable size, a new life-planet system is started for an interstellar region.

Two fundamental principles of Universe governance form a paradox. On the one hand, the Universe is consciously evolved by decentralized, advanced civilizations. The principle of decentralized exopolitical evolution governs the development of intelligent civilizations in the Universe. On the other hand, source maintains ultimate centralized control over all reality. In this way, creation of the Universe is both centralized in one source, and decentralized in many multi-dimensional civilizations.

There is a deeper, dimensional structure to the Universe. We humans are accustomed to thinking of a physical Universe composed of such basic natural building blocks as solar systems and galaxies. Universe government cuts across such natural phenomena as solar systems and galaxies, and extends beyond the interstellar space we visually see. The Universe is a living, evolving entity, composed of many dimensions and realities. Universe society functions beyond physical interstellar space, and throughout the multiplicity of Universe realties and dimensions.

As holographic fragments of a living Universe, we humans are ourselves multi-dimensional beings. Humans exist in overlapping dimensions. Our physical bodies and our spiritual souls function together, but in radically different dimensions of the Universe. Think of Earth and its planetary network as our "body politic" and our network capital as our "planetary soul."

Like the body and soul of a human being, networks of Universe government co-exist in radically different dimensions of the Universe. The principle of over-lapping multi-dimensionality applies as well to the design of Universe governmental Exopolitics. Universe society has its governmental capitals, much as Earth's governmental systems do. The capital of Earth's planetary network is located within another Universe dimension, invisible to our current human science.

Earth's political systems are built around geographical "capitals" where the interactive business of government takes place in judicial, legislative, and executive forums. By contrast, the "capitals" of our interplanetary networks are located within dimensions of the Universe that Earth has yet to discover. Planetary network capitals are located within older, more evolved dimensions of the Universe than the planets – like Earth – that it oversees. The Universe itself evolves, including the multiplicity of its innermost, most advanced dimensions, as well as the familiar dimension of "outer space."

Our interplanetary capital is more "spiritual" in nature than its member planets, such as Earth. Our planetary capital is located within a more spiritual dimension than the interstellar space that we know. Our capital carries out government and politics by means of advanced Universe technologies of dimensionality and reflectivity.

We planets are in a "virtual reality." The location of our network capital is "virtual," or in some more advanced dimensional realm, that our fragmentary religious traditions may call "Heaven." The capital's virtual "location" in another dimension facilitates its oversight of both the physical and spiritual evolution of life-bearing planets in its jurisdiction.

We must be fearless in letting go of erroneous concepts embedded in our science and religious traditions if we are to understand how the Universe evolves intelligent life. We carry unnecessary emotional and conceptual baggage as to how life-bearing planets are grown and organized. Think of the Universe as a vast and growing Mind, endlessly creating from its central source, yet decentralized in its architecture and operations.

As individuals, we are actually part of that universal mind. The ultimate source of the Universe is a person inside the Universe (as each of us is). The source is the evolving Universe itself as well. A living, holographic fragment of source is within each of our souls. These are all aspects of the source (known as God).

As we evolve more fully, we may actually come to meet source, face-to-face, within a dimensional world at the central point of the known Universe. This very real, dimensional location is known in our religious traditions as "Paradise," the center of "Heaven." Our current human science does not have the tools to understand or perceive this ultimate Universe dimension.

The Universe is the most imaginative thriller known. The exquisite design of the intelligent Universe focuses on the growth of our individual souls. The soul is our non-temporal navigator through the myriad dimensions of the Universe.

You can think of our planet Earth and the whole system of life-bearing planets as a greenhouse for growing souls. One goal of source is to share its Universe with beings who can themselves evolve eventually into source-like beings. Ultimately, the facts of science and the concepts of religion actually do merge as we evolve in this Universe that we inhabit.

There are perceptual barriers and doorways to humanity's acquisition of its next level of universal knowledge. We will not be able to "see" the structure of Universe society, our life-bearing planet neighbours, until we are ready. We cannot rush this process of our reintegration into Universe society. But we can create the conditions and social permission on Earth for our civilization and Universe society to interact in a shared reality. Admission to interplanetary society may require that we openly acknowledge Earth as an isolated planetary member.

To use another metaphor, we on Earth are in a mystery school. The mystery school is the Universe itself. Our human history and evolution is actually an unfolding tour, so deeply guided as to be beyond the comprehension of our mortal intellects. The goal of this mystery tour is our growth as non-temporal beings. The source creates this Universe mystery school, and guides us through stages of planetary evolution.

Earth's mystery school is designed to prevent the human community from venturing outward into the Universe without first becoming aware of its intelligent and moral order. To integrate with Universe society, we need to transform ourselves into open citizens of Universe society. Without such a transformation, our community will not even become aware that it is in a populated and ordered intelligent Universe. Instead, Earth would remain within its planetary isolation, in an evolutionary cul-de-sac.

Federal systems of government here on Earth reflect the design of Universe government. Under a decentralized federal system, a hierarchy of federal governments controls local governments. The design of federal governments on Earth is actually a holographic reflection of Universe-based governments. Local networks of life-bearing planets are under the jurisdiction of "federal" Universe capitals located deeper within dimensions of the Universe which humanity cannot presently perceive.

From their more evolved, spiritual dimensions, these federal Universe capitals oversee vast interplanetary federations. Government on these Universe capitals is analogous to the primitive governmental forms we craft on Earth. The legislative, judicial, and executive functions we know of Earth all are derived via hologram from the design of Universe government. Earth's governmental forms are flawed because of the heritage of our planetary quarantine. Our governments are primitive because humanity is a very, very young intelligent species in the Universe.

Think of Universe capitals as being analogous to state or provincial capitals on Earth. Basic legislative, executive, and judicial powers are exercised on Universe capitals, as they are at state and provincial capitals on Earth. Universe capitals serve as inter-dimensional legislatures, where the laws and statutes of Universe society are politicked, debated, formulated, and enacted.

The Universe executive branch is analogous to a state governor or provincial premier. A Universe executive establishes its seat of governmental authority at these inter-dimensional capitals. The executive functions of Universe government include overseeing the development and evolution of the life-bearing planets, and keeping the peace of Universe society.

Think of Universe executives as highly advanced "god-beings" with powers of Universe creation, and authority over quadrants of universal reality. Traditional Earth religions often refer to Universe executives as the "gods" or "God."

Universe courts are located throughout the various federal levels of Universe government, dispensing justice under public and private universal law. Among the many issues that these courts adjudicate, for example, are orders for the isolation or quarantine of errant planets, such as Earth.

Earth is now in political isolation, and does not participate directly in

Universe government. In effect, we have defaulted on our Universe privileges, including that of self-government. The more advanced and evolved civilizations tend to be more involved in Universe governance.

As a civilization advances in spiritual evolution, it also advances in governmental power and authority within the Universe. This connection between spiritual and political power is a phenomenon of universal law and planetary evolution. An advanced civilization possesses a sense of cosmic responsibility, and can oversee the creation and development of new intelligent planetary life. Our human community has been isolated from our cosmic heritage. Rejoining Universe society will help us reacquire our cosmic responsibilities. In turn, a cosmic sense will nourish our evolution as a community of spiritual beings

Politics, then, does not stop at Earth's edge. In fact, it appears that the higher we proceed within the Universe community, the more comprehensive is the scope of Universe Exopolitics. Consider the political dynamics operating at the Universe capital overseeing our planetary isolation. We can surmise that powerful Universe forces support our reintegration into interplanetary society.

Earth's quarantine is the result of an extended governance process, analogous to a traumatic international political and governmental process on Earth – for example, World War II. The specific conditions of our planetary isolation are contained in legislative statutes, executive regulations, and judicial case decisions of Universe government. Our emergence from planetary quarantine will be as much dictated by Universe government, as was our original isolation.

Universal law is the blueprint for politics, government, and law on Earth. Universe justice and law are embedded in the deeper design of Earth's governmental structures. Earth's governmental forms – legislative, executive, and judicial – have the potential to guide Earth into integration with Universe society. Earth's governments need only be openly oriented toward Universe integration.

In turn, the initiatives of Universe government impact us here on Earth. Our predisposition to re-integrate Earth into interplanetary society grows, even as we are not fully aware of the forces supporting our Universe reunion. Universe government guides us from its multiple dimensions, through the barriers and obstacles to our interplanetary reunion.

Universe government extends inward to spiritual dimensions that are even more evolved than interplanetary capitals. At the more advanced capitals of Universe government, creation and government merge. Universe executives here take on the creative functions – literally – of "gods." These advanced executive beings can bring entire new physical quadrants of the Universe into being. They establish governance processes, and develop these new, organic quadrants of space. Universe executives oversee the development of this new reality over billions of years and cultivate entire systems of life-bearing planets.

The inner structure of the Universe may well be created and overseen by evolving "god-beings." Human science does not yet know these secrets, but fragments of secret knowledge about the inner structure survive in human religions. Universe politics plays out on multiple levels here on Earth. Some exopolitical issues are so profound that their resolution requires direct intervention by "god-beings." More routine issues of Exopolitics are resolved through the decentralized authority of Universe legislation, judicial decisions, or executive enforcement.

Earth's Exopolitics are unusual in the Universe. Our status as an isolated planet is officially unknown to us. Yet our reintegration into Universe society depends on our becoming collectively aware of our isolation. To end our isolation, a critical mass of us must be aware that Earth is part of a populated, advanced, organized interplanetary society. Human beliefs about extraterrestrial reality must expand beyond their present limits. Our next planetary frontier consists of a critical mass of humanity becoming collectively aware of, and openly part of, Universe society.

The evolution, development, and government of the Universe are decentralized. A single, common source, however, maintains the vastness of the outer worlds of inhabited space and the inner dimensions of Universe governance and creation. That original source is a being or process or energy called Yahweh, Dios, Dieux, Allah, and the other names of God found in the world's sacred religious traditions.

God is the ultimate political being in the Universe. The complexity of the Creator is such that we can hardly comprehend God's very multiplicity. At the transcendent level, God is the Universe as it evolves. At a more immanent level, a personal being God resides at the most central administrative capital within the entire Universe.

This central exopolitical capital, known in some human religious concepts as "Paradise," is – scientifically – the ultimate source of all life, intelligence, and spirit that exists. Given the correct spiritual circumstances, each of us could come face-to-face with the personal God at this central Paradise. A holographic particle of God resides within the intelligent, spiritual beings of the Universe. This is what makes the human soul divine.

The principles of the Universe politics ultimately govern our politics on Earth. Earth's political institutions – flawed by our quarantine – are based on Universe politics. It may surprise you that political institutions analogous to those here on Earth should govern an advanced and complex Universe. Universe politics seem far away from Earthly stereotypes of troubled religious institutions and corrupt politics. Advanced justice, laws, courts, legislatures, and governmental executives exist out in the vastness of the Universe. Universe government is the source for all human political institutions, as they struggle out of our Universe isolation.

No wonder human science lacks the tools for developing insight into intelligent life in the Universe. Exobiology, the study of the possibility of extraterrestrial life, is our contemporary tool for studying extraterrestrial life. The focus of exobiology is the micro-organism, a fundamental building block of life. Exobiology in its present form seeks to establish the conditions of micro-organic alien life. It studies specialized planetary conditions so as to discover if conditions for primitive life forms have arisen.

Exoarchaeology is the scientific study of sites and artefacts associated with space exploration that humans are creating both on Earth and off-world on other celestial bodies, such as the Moon and Mars, or on artificial satellites. Exoarchaeology is also the scientific study of sites and artefacts associated with intelligent off-planet cultures, created on celestial bodies within the Solar System, such as the Moon and Mars, or on any celestial body or artificial satellite in the Universe.

Together, the interrelated disciplines of Exobiology, Exoarchaeology, and Exopolitics (the study of politics, government, and law in the Universe) are necessary for the study of the off-planet cultures of intelligent civilizations in the Universe, and for reintegrating our human society with a larger, organized Universe society. Our scientific establishment has a deep-seated, antagonistic bias against acknowledging the existence of more advanced civilizations in Earth's environment. Clearly, the paradigms of science must be transformed if we humans are to integrate into larger Universe society.

A transformed Exobiology, Exoarchaeology, and Exopolitics would construct a bridge of knowledge and relationship with advanced civilizations in the Universe. The scientific enemies of Universe society have had their historical day and failed. In 1939, physicist Enrico Fermi stated his famous paradox – if Universe civilizations exist, then why have they not already visited Earth? Fermi's approach is doubly bankrupt. Universe civilizations have not "officially" appeared precisely because the Earth is in legal quarantine. Universe civilizations, however, are in daily, profound, and permanent contact with Earth's ecology. They oversee our planet and its evolution and raise the consciousness of the collective human mind.

Universe civilizations do not visit Earth episodically. They are a permanent part of Earth's ecology. Earth is a life experiment project of Universe society, and is under Universe politics and governance. Our interplanetary capital is Earth's closest level of Universe government. Like local governments on Earth, local planetary capitals focus on broad issues of planetary welfare, as well as on the biological and spiritual status of intelligent life.

Earth is a life experiment planet, and *homo sapiens* is a life experiment species. Universe scientists, who continue to monitor biological and evolutionary conditions on Earth, biologically engineer humans to some degree. Intervention in human evolution takes place under minimal interference rules for life-bearing planets. Monitoring facilitates Universe society's control of the decentralized processes of planetary evolutionary.

These twin evolutionary principles – planetary non-intervention and planetary over-control – may seem mutually contradictory and paradoxical. This apparent contradiction can be resolved through different Universe standards. Control over evolution is activated when the very existence of a desired evolutionary end is threatened.

We exist in a Universe that is simultaneously "physical" and "spiritual," and there is no fundamental contradiction between the two. The "physical" aspects of the Universe are its newer, less real creations, and the Universe's "spiritual" aspects are its older, more real dimensions. These physical and spiritual aspects are along a spectrum of creation, consciousness, and energy. It is misleading to describe Universe government as an interplanetary federation, and not include its dimensional, spiritual aspects of governance.

Higher Universe levels of government are responsible for the unification and stabilization of the vast systems of life-bearing planets under their jurisdiction. Planetary unification includes integration of life-bearing planets into interplanetary society. Planetary stabilization relates to the relative social, political, and spiritual status of a life-bearing planet such as Earth. Planetary stability is of high concern in the case of quarantined planets such as Earth.

The turmoil experienced on quarantined planets such as Earth conceals an inner truth. Universe governance closely monitors social and evolutionary conditions on life-bearing planets. The precise conditions triggering a planetary intervention may be very difficult for us to discern. We do not know with certainty why Earth's quarantine has been allowed to continue for so long, with its historical legacy of war, poverty, ignorance, disease, and the sum of human suffering.

Obviously, there is more to know, as the perspective of higher Universe government extends over epochs lasting billions of years and more. Universe government is a deep mystery at this stage, as are its interventions into a quarantined planet. Oversight of a quarantined planet such as Earth is challenging, as the Universe administration must remain officially invisible.

Consciousness communication circuits are one of the mechanisms by which Universe society acts invisibly on Earth. Circuits of Universe consciousness can communicate desired cosmic insights, information, and inspiration to key individuals and society-at-large on a quarantined planet. For example, Universe consciousness circuits may be used to cultivate planetary attitudes where "war" and "poverty" are unacceptable as social conditions.

There are stages to the development of life-bearing planets. Earth is about to reach that evolutionary stage where war and poverty are abolished. In Earth's case, were Earth to be openly re-integrated with Universe society, conflict resolution techniques and free energy production technology would abolish war and poverty on a global basis. The technology of "free energy" leads to a demise of the petroleum and nuclear civilization and the elite power structure that enforces and benefits from it. Open integration with Universe society would enforce universal disarmament and the end of war as legally sanctioned murder.

If human civilization does not acquire mass access to cosmic energy sources, the petroleum and nuclear-based power structure of Earth might endure, with the top 250 families and individuals on Earth owning more wealth than the bottom 2.5 billion persons do. One formula for maintaining Earth's isolation might consist of increasing the already obscene concentration of power and wealth, while keeping humanity ignorant about Universe society. Our ultimate liberation will depend largely on how Exopolitics can free our institutions from the grip of these plutocracies.

The highest levels of Universe government are most concerned with the spiritual evolution of interstellar space, its vast networks of life-bearing planets, and its myriad civilizations of intelligent, spiritual beings. Earth has been the subject of special scrutiny within the higher universal realms. In our history as a planet, we have been quarantined primarily for spiritual reasons. Hence, within Universe society, Earth is an unusual and fairly well known life experiment planet. Metaphorically, Earth is the Galapagos Islands of spiritual evolution, because the species of souls we produce are greatly affected by our isolation.

Parascience now confirms the existence of such energy entities as the human aura, spirit, and soul. Our physical bodies are nestled within an energy complex known as an aura, with cosmic energy gates known as "chakras," from their sacred religious name. Our biological bodies eventually die. Our non-temporal souls, however, survive and evolve in an eternal universal adventure. After bodily death, evolving human souls inhabit the more real, spiritual dimensions of universal reality. Humans are of an evolutionary class of intelligent beings, as are many of the beings populating the civilizations in the vast networks of inhabited planets.

The governmental structure of Universe society is relatively simple yet complex enough to deal with the multiplicity of dimensions and issues that come before it. Universe government's judicial function is far-flung, and has multiple levels of jurisdiction. Evolving beings from intelligent civilizations can become judges in Universe courts that extend throughout its dimensions. These courts deal with important issues, such as the readmission of isolated planets and governmental crimes by highly placed executives within the Universe. Evolving souls like us can be part of Universe legislative bodies and set standards for life-bearing planets.

Because of our history of planetary isolation, human souls from Earth may be temporarily underrepresented in the current structure of Universe government. Once we overtly reintegrate with Universe society, these channels of participation will more readily open to us, for a profound order lies beneath this governmental structure.

Our human culture is such that we expect a useful career will be limited to a single human life span of 65 to 80 years. In fact, our Universe careers are limitless, and the opportunities for growth, evolution, and service are both profound and multiple. Bodily death on this planet is, in scientific terms, but a transition to a more real and fulfilling level of universal reality. Our corrupted knowledge – the untoward product of our planetary isolation – has treated death and the afterlife with fear and superstition.

"As above, so below" is a useful metaphor in understanding the structure of Universe society. Despite our isolation, the basic design of Universe structures – the "above" reality – is still mirrored here on Earth, the "below" reality. The basic underlying designs of Universe society are present on every life-bearing planet. Planetary reality is indelibly interconnected, through inter-dimensional space, and inward to the common source of the evolving Universe that we inhabit.

Interplanetary governance is reflected in the science fiction stereotypes of our literature, films, television shows, and popular culture. Some popular literature and cinema capture the spirit of multi-dimensional Universe society more readily than others. Culture, music, films, books, and art are important modalities for raising universal awareness on Earth.

Universe society maintains an operating network of communication, diplomacy, and culture among its integrated planets. Interplanetary networks are subject to a complex of Universe laws, regulations, and enforcement mechanisms. Everything from interplanetary travel to the requirements for interplanetary regulation is set out by federation-network rules. Earth's international laws, as well as its institutions, treaties, and regulations governing everything from diplomacy to air flight, are a mirror reflection of these Universe rules.

Universe government is particularly concerned with reintegrating isolated planets like Earth that have been quarantined. Planets isolated in this manner may lack a planetary governmental, political, and social infrastructure necessary to participate in interplanetary society. Very often the planetary stages of global integration cannot be rushed, and reintegration of isolated planets must come in lengthy stages.

Earth is part of an ancient, epochal community of life-bearing planets. Our planetary community has a far-flung network of communication and interplanetary representation. Planetary self-government and its members are as diverse as universal reality itself. Patience may be one of the key evolutionary qualities of intelligent beings incarnating on isolated worlds like Earth. Think of the individual and collective traumas experienced in the last century – global wars, totalitarian dictatorships, genocide, and political and social oppression. This is the evolutionary baseline Earth has endured as a consequence of planetary quarantine.

Earth's religions are ultimately right, however, about the structure of Universe politics. In fact, God rules the entire Universe through government. The governance of Universe society is decentralized and yet ultimately proceeds from the original source of all reality – God.

The relationship between universal governmental forms and terrestrial governmental forms is far deeper than mere comparative government. It is holographic. As noted above, a hologram is an entity in which the whole of the hologram is present in every part of the hologram. Universal government is holographic in the sense that the whole of the Universe government appears in its every part. Terrestrial natural law, social law, and constitutional law are actual holographic entities of universal law. That is why we have justice as a principle of jurisprudence (improperly applied since the planetary cataclysmic rebellion and the quarantine). The whole (universal law) is contained in the part (terrestrial law).

Very roughly speaking, the legislative pattern of Universe government can be seen in Earth's legislatures, even corrupted as they are from the planetary quarantine. The executive function of Universe government is reflected in Earth's political structures. Concepts such as "the divine right of kings" and "the emperor as divinity personified" are cultural leftovers from a distant human memory of the divine aspects of Universe government.

Our science fiction novels, films, and TV shows have made interplanetary federation familiar to us. We can readily understand how an interplanetary federation might work. Likewise, we can understand the concept of a Universe judiciary. Universe courts decide disputes among planets. Universe courts and legislatures are the holographic models for legislatures and courts on Earth. We can understand them because evolving humans are included as judges and legislators. Universe judges include evolving souls from diverse planets in the interplanetary federation.

The executive function of Universe government is mysterious. The rulers of the Universe are gods – beings with the power of creation who have earned the right to create and oversee their own quadrants of universal reality. There is a difference between acknowledging gods in the Universe and acknowledging the existence of extraterrestrial civilizations.

Science stereotypically rejects the possibility that God exists. The existence of interplanetary legislatures might be a subject for scientific, empirical research. The existence of God and sons of God – the factual creators and rulers of the Universe – is the subject of religious disagreement, scientific controversy, and popular confusion.

We humans intimately participate in the executive governance of the Universe, through inner spiritual circuits. Each level of Universe government is under the oversight of an advanced "god-being," with ultimate authority over all planetary governments, local Universe creations, and the evolving Universe itself.

Each of us has a holographic entity of God within us, as does each spiritual entity in the Universe. In each of us you will find the whole (God), and in the whole (God) you will find the part (we humans). We can influence events in the Universe through conscious spiritual acts. This is not metaphor, but actual reality.

Earth has been long disconnected from Universe government. Reintegration with Universe society will bring us into contact with the network of fellow planets. Integration will also reconnect Earth to cosmic circuits of divinity, to a higher plane of conscious perception, to the divine aspects of Universe structure and government. The process of reintegration will be gradual and will proceed in stages. It is, however, a reclaiming of our original blueprint as divinely connected, evolving beings.

7

Exopolitics: Humans are as Humans Do

EARTH HAS BEEN LONG absent from open participation in the community of life-bearing planets. We lack interplanetary capabilities, ranging from adequate universal awareness, to the advanced technologies for interplanetary communication, travel, diplomacy, and commerce. War is the principal method of conflict resolution, as well as the resource and industrial base of our petroleum-nuclear civilization.

Military and intelligence behemoths consume a disproportionate percentage of national wealth. They corrupt our politics, economies, and societies. Hidden new military technologies, based on scalar energy, electromagnetic pulse energy, and other systems, are now deployed for unspeakable environmental warfare, as well as mind control operations against Earth's people.

Universe politics on Earth is a legacy from our original isolation. This legacy explains the persistence of evil, oppression, deceit, duplicity, and conflict in human politics and political arrangements. The planetary quarantine has left us with a legacy of unethical political intrigue.

Base cunning underlies the political decision to cover up ongoing approaches by extraterrestrial civilizations over the last 50 years. Patterns of our original planetary quarantine continue even until the present. The causes of the quarantine are being repeated as unconscious, dysfunctional social patterns in present-day human culture. They can be found in the destructive, self-serving agendas of covert networks hidden within Earth's academic, military, industrial, governmental, and political establishments, as well as the more selfish of its plutocracies.

If we concluded that these military and intelligence forces were acting unconsciously, there might be grounds to forgive them for the destruction that they are causing. Yet the evidence shows that the information war against Universe society is quite deliberate. Similarly, we might forgive the military and intelligence forces if they were sincere in a mistaken belief that extraterrestrial civilizations intend to destroy human society. Yet, the evidence shows that Universe civilizations are signalling their positive role.

Earth's integration into interplanetary society depends on how we ourselves act. All politics are local, global, and ultimately universal. Human avarice, violence, arrogance, and emptiness can impact on our relationships with Universe society. If we remain a regressive human society, this will only lengthen our isolation in the Universe.

The Universe politics game on Earth is convoluted and covert. Major secret terrestrial networks knowingly keep Earth in the dark about our Universe heritage. These forces consciously keep humanity isolated from the rest of the Universe. Their war-like, destructive behaviour is grossly immoral and hard to countenance. These major covert players are intentionally continuing the cycle of Universe isolation that has been in effect on Earth since our original planetary quarantine.

Is our generation – in the early 21st century – going to be the one to end this cycle of isolation? Perhaps. Whether or not our isolation is ended will all depend on the processes of Universe politics. Integration into interplanetary society is interactive, and requires a motivated human race seeking entry into Universe society.

The challenges of Universe integration are daunting. They start with the destructive politics of planetary isolation. Since the mid-20th century, secret networks spanning intelligence, military, and economic organizations have waged a global information war to keep humanity confused about extraterrestrial contact. Their goal has been to maintain planetary secrecy about Universe society. By way of this planetary secrecy, they, firstly, reinforce their illegitimate power over human society, secondly, prevent humanity from becoming politically conscious of its potential choice to join Universe society, and thirdly, appropriate advanced Universe technologies and advantages for their own selfish purposes.

Universe politics is a process whose goal is the liberation of Earth from this captivity. On the other side of the terrestrial military-industrial complex are the forces of Universe society, subtly awakening a critical mass of humanity to a Universe consciousness. Ultimately, this aware humanity may act as a political counterweight, allowing humanity to choose re-entry into Universe society.

There is a spiritual dimension to the process of Exopolitics. "We are gods in the making" is a truth that well applies to the community of human souls, as they evolve spiritually over long Universe careers. Universe politics contains issues we would normally call "religious" or "spiritual." Religious traditions on Earth may, in fact, be historical accounts of occasions when "the gods" or representatives of extraterrestrial civilizations visited Earth. As Earth opens to Universe society, we may come to experience that Universe civilizations are composed of evolving spiritual beings.

Intelligent life in the Universe reflects a deep and dramatic cosmic unfolding that has an exopolitical as well as a spiritual context. Human religious traditions are built around the incarnations of spiritual beings of the stature of Buddha, Mohammed, and Jesus, whose lives have both spiritual and exopolitical impacts. Beings of high spiritual stature incarnate on Earth as part of their existential development, as well as to aid in the development of humanity. Exopolitically, each of these incarnations can be seen as a step in the ultimate reintegration of Earth into Universe society in the aftermath of the rebellion and planetary quarantine. If the Earth is, in fact (as some religious traditions hold), an arena for "god-being" incarnations, we can speculate that the timing of Earth's re-entry into open Universe politics may be part of an extended cosmic drama. The same advanced evolving "god-beings" that imposed our quarantine may now be directing the Universe integration of the planet.

The Universe politics of the last 50 years may have been the "last gasp" of the forces of darkness, of the original planetary quarantine on Earth. Since the middle of the 20th century, a covert executive network has, for its own power, secretly controlled the management of Earth's interactions with extraterrestrial civilizations. These executive networks have been in a state of active war against the Universe administration. As a result, humanity has been excluded from participating in its Universe heritage.

Universe politics is an historical and evolutionary spiral. In the same way that a militaristic plutocracy "caused" the original isolation of Earth, our current militaristic plutocracy is attempting to continue the quarantine and their ultimately illusory control over Earth's civilization.

Let us expand this perspective. Suppose Universe society has been knowingly gaming with this militaristic plutocracy, with the goal of ultimately liberating humanity.

In the current phase of their "gaming" to bring humanity into universal awareness, Universe governance pursues a multi-dimensional strategy, which involves raising humanity's consciousness and political will to integrate with interplanetary society. This strategy is carried out through an integrated outreach to Earth, including large-scale psychological conditioning projects, like the UFO phenomenon. Psy ops are the modality that this secret Earth force has used to keep humanity captive from the Universe society's current wave of approach.

Conversely, progressive Universe politics are open, transparent, creative, and resourceful. There is a human force attempting to mobilize humanity into integration with Universe society. It is a diverse, grassroots lobby for our collective future. This citizen's lobby is a vanguard for our collective evolution.

We must involve our bodies politic in the process of achieving reunion with the Universe. A large part of the official deception and secrecy about Universe society is designed precisely to keep our body politic inert and apathetic about our interplanetary heritage. We need to activate universal awareness, and break through to interaction with Universe society.

Breaking through to Universe society is about community politics. Integration with Universe society comes about when a critical mass of humanity achieves the political will to seek its Universe heritage. Ours is a time to commit our individual beings, and our awareness, to our cosmic citizenship. Playing Universe politics is based on trusting our inner judgment and intuition. By activating our cosmic bodies politic, we can deconstruct terrestrial manipulation and deception and forge a positive future for humanity in interplanetary society.

PART THREE

A Decade of Contact

HOW EXOPOLITICS IS THE best strategy to exit our planetary quarantine. How as a central act of Exopolitics, humanity should create the Decade of Contact, a 10-year social program officially dedicated to examining the issues of extraterrestrial contact, a decade of official world participation in activating global consciousness and knowledge about Universe society.

8

The Infancy of Exopolitics

EXOPOLITICS, THE STUDY OF political process and governance in interstellar society, is in its infancy. Yet Exopolitics is a key channel to transforming our human future. One immediate action program of Exopolitics is a decade of human education and community politics directed towards integration with Universe society – the Decade of Contact.

The Decade of Contact is a social program to examine the issues of extraterrestrial contact, a decade of official world participation in activating global consciousness and knowledge about Universe society. The goals of the Decade of Contact include the implementation of Exopolitics on Earth, and the study of Earth's role in Universe government and politics. Through education, media, and grass roots politics, a Decade of Contact can bring awareness to public consciousness about Universe society, and can reorient human science and institutions to be "extraterrestrial friendly."

Earth is only one of countless populated planets in an organized Universe that is under the guidance of an advanced Universe society. A near majority of the human population intuitively knows the truth. Extraterrestrial civilizations visit Earth, and an interplanetary federation governs Earth itself. Humanity does not know of or see this Universe government, because Earth has been under deliberate quarantine, isolated from the rest of interstellar society.

Human religious traditions and emerging sciences like scientific remote viewing may contain fragmentary information about the catastrophic disruption in our exopolitical past. We do not yet accurately know the full, official reasons for our planetary quarantine by the Universe. It may turn out to be the case that Earth has been quarantined for solely evolutionary reasons, as a planet not yet advanced enough for social interaction with the rest of Universe society. Perhaps a "minimal interference" rule may be in force, whereby more advanced civilizations are prohibited from interfering with a less-evolved Universe civilization.

The pattern of evidence supports the Exopolitics model. Cumulatively, recent scientific analysis of the extraterrestrial Leaky Embargo strategy, the inner consistency among human religious traditions about the myth of "humanity's fall from the Garden of Eden," and scientific remote viewing data confirming the historical accuracy of exopolitical versions of a catastrophic planetary rebellion, all converge to reinforce why the Exopolitics model may be our new dominant universal paradigm. Earth has been quarantined for essentially exopolitical reasons – reasons of Universe law or politics. Earth has indeed suffered a severe violation of interplanetary norms in the distant past, and now must prove itself worthy of membership in the body politic of the Universe.

We humans are historical victims of Universe politics in the sense that, to date, humanity has not been deemed ready to resume Universe citizenship and the exopolitical game. Ask yourself these "what if" questions, which relate to extricating ourselves from universal isolation:

- What if our planet Earth is part of an organized society of inhabited planets?

- What if we have been kept deliberately ignorant, and in quarantine?

- What if the key to reintegrating us with our fellow planets lies in our own power to change our society?

- What if we can become ready for Universe citizenship, and Universe politics?

- What if there are steps we humans can take to make our universal reunion happen?

The human transformation brought by addressing these questions would be profound. If Earth is part of a well-governed Universe, then our entire human civilization – including our governance, our technology, and our ways of life – could be transformed. The discovery that we are not alone, but are part of an organized society, would be the greatest single transformation in the long history of humanity – greater than any previous scientific, political, or social shift.

Re-entry into Universe society would mean that substantial aspects of contemporary human life must be changed. Our re-entry into interplanetary society would be an evolutionary quantum leap. Our evolutionary blueprint is as an interstellar species. As a practical matter, we could actualize this blueprint only as part of organized interstellar society. As we broke through our universal isolation, we would be ejecting millennia of social and emotional baggage in our awakening to Universe citizenship.

Every morning, 6.5 billion human beings wake up to a false or incomplete story of who we are. Our conventional history tells us that we are the only intelligent species in the entire Universe. Our collective intuition tells us differently, that we live in a populated Universe. A majority of US adults tells us that we are not alone in the vastness of space. The scientifically measured intuitions of between 50 and 100 million US adults seem to know that we are part of a highly organized interplanetary society. Presumably, an equal proportion of the rest of the world's population also knows this intuitively. Yet for evolutionary and political reasons, humanity seems to have been deliberately kept officially in the dark.

9

A User's Guide to Life

IT IS LITTLE WONDER that there is so much confusion on this planet about our role in the larger Universe. Our personal confusion starts at birth. Our parents, who themselves have been confused all their lives about the universal role of this planet, pass on their own programming to us. As we grow up, more confusion comes our way from our schools, religions, governments, institutions, media, and peers. We ourselves eventually become transmitters of confusion, and pass more advanced universal confusion on to our peers, families, friends, and children.

How much easier and less confusing life might be if we each were issued a User's Guide to Life, at birth, one that would be updated in real time. A User's Guide to Life for every human being on the planet would contain standard instructions for at least four elements of our life on Earth:

1. How most of the story modern human beings know about Earth and its environs is wrong.

2. How it is most logical and rational that we live in a highly populous and organized Universe society of life-bearing planets.

3. How Universe politics have kept Earth in a planetary quarantine.

4. How that quarantine may be lifting, and what we can do to hasten a universal reunion.

A User's Guide to Life would reassess and contradict key tenets of contemporary human civilization about the universal circumstances of Planet Earth. Paradoxically, each of humanity's contemporary worldviews, from creationist to evolutionist, contains an element of truth about the origin and structure of the Cosmos. Our User's Guide to Life would show how every dominant cosmology humans now espouse about the relationship of

Earth to the Universe is wrong or incomplete – humanity is, in fact, not alone in the Universe.

Interplanetary society may not come as much of a surprise to the 50 to 100 million extraterrestrial-sensitive persons in the United States. If you are one of the extraterrestrial-curious elsewhere on the planet, you may likewise see the Universe in its true, populated interconnectedness.

In an evolutionary sense, the ability to see that this planet is under "invisible" extraterrestrial political and administrative control means that you have probably activated your Universe consciousness. Your extraterrestrial-friendly vision is somewhat like the vision of round Earth believers during the flat Earth era.

Science, not religion, is the archetypal discipline for exploring space. Religion, however, as an expression of the collective human intuition, may be one of our more fruitful access points to working models for the study of intelligent civilizations in interstellar space. Exobiology and Exopolitics contain ancient, modern, and emerging disciplines for the study of the Universe. The disciplines of human religious traditions – Judaism, Christianity, Islam, Buddhism, Hinduism, and the approximately 4,000 other human religions – contain ancient and potentially fruitful models of the first principles under which the Universe is organized.

Religion was humanity's first science and its first cosmology. Sacred, religious models of intelligent life in the Universe are a starting point. Religion is the repository of the collective intuitive reality. It often claims to be influenced or created by a higher intelligence. We can trust this collective intuition, and guide it with the principles of the scientific method.

The truth is that our Universe is filled with intelligent civilizations. In fact, advanced civilizations consciously participate in the continued evolution of our Universe. The vast expanse of interstellar space may appear ordered to you, but devoid of other intelligent life. Our contemporary science tells us the physical Universe appears ordered because it is ruled by the natural laws described in physics, astrophysics, astronomy, and related physical sciences. Biased science holds that our cosmic reality is devoid of other intelligent life.

We on Earth do not officially recognize that our Universe is populated and organized because:

1. Our inability to perceive higher civilizations in our universal environment is an illusion, an evolutionary mask, deliberately crafted by interplanetary society. Earth is under Universe quarantine imposed by the interplanetary government. We have not been allowed to interact overtly with other civilizations. This has had profound effects on our perceptions of our world.

2. Humanity has not been able to perceive other intelligent civilizations in the past because we are only now evolving to the stage of acquiring the science necessary to locate other intelligent civilizations. We simply have not known how and where to find other civilizations.

3. The Universe may appear to humans as devoid of intelligent life because we are not yet able to understand or perceive the ongoing signals from and visitations of extraterrestrial civilizations on Earth.

4. Our perception of extraterrestrial visits is blocked by covert intelligence agencies and other human factions wanting to keep Earth isolated from the rest of interstellar society for their own reasons. One way of psychologically blocking human perception of Universe society is to inundate humanity with misleading and misinforming UFO "sightings" and phoney "alien abduction" accounts.

Each of these factors is a potent force that keeps Earth physically and psychologically isolated from Universe society.

The laws of physics, astrophysics, and astronomy represent only one mode of determining the true realities and dynamics of the Universe. Universal law is even more fundamental to the workings of the physical Universe than are the laws of physics, astrophysics, and astronomy. Humanity's evolutionary circumstances and exopolitical status are subject to Universe law. The ancient models of the world's religions and philosophies also provide very suggestive models for Exopolitics.

A more appropriate approach to Universe society is the intuitive method of knowledge. This intuitive approach to our Universe is not what the contemporary human scientific establishment wants us to pursue. Since time immemorial, our human culture has used intuition to survive. Our User's Guide uses the inductive, intuitive method to build a working model of what the Universe is really like.

As you study Exopolitics, try constructing your own working model of the Universe government. Use your own intuition to evaluate whether Earth is part of an interplanetary society of advanced civilizations. Your own intuition, together with the revelations of humanity's great religions, can suggest key aspects of Universe society.

There is one way you can create dramatic personal change in your life on this planet. Let go of the illusion that outer space is empty and devoid of organized intelligent society. Let go of the illusion that there is no organized Universe society monitoring Earth now. In letting go of your false illusions about Planet Earth's isolation, you can develop a more natural relationship to your own full Universe heritage.

Grasp hold of your intuition. It is as powerful as your intellect, if not more powerful. Let your intuition wander freely over the vision of a populated and regulated Universe, with travel and commerce among life-bearing planets, with interplanetary organizations, universities, and communications media. Visualize planetary societies and intelligent species that may differ widely in their evolution.

Visualize the workings of an interstellar federation of planets. Every school child on Earth knows that interplanetary federations mean interstellar government, laws, and politics. Interplanetary government directives are under universal law, the rudimentary workings of which we humans can understand. Universe courts and administrative tribunals adjudicate conflicts under Universe government directives. Universe officials use the enforcement technology of interplanetary society to carry out universal law.

On the surface, Universe government functions much the same as governmental bodies and courts do on Earth. That is because Earth is under universal law, and terrestrial government is derived from Universe government. Human culture is currently unaware of its Universe heritage, which provides the blueprint for our Earthly institutions.

Your intuition can help you access knowledge about Universe society, knowledge that can lead to your personal liberation. Your intuition can understand the basics of how Universe society functions. Your intuition can lead to the realization that interplanetary space is populated. The Universe has a government which functions according to principles we on Earth can understand.

10

Spiritual and Material Reality

AS THE SOCIETY OF a life-bearing planet matures and evolves, it comes to understand the Universe as a sacred realm. Understanding that the Universe is sacred and spiritual in nature is fundamental to the evolution of a higher intelligent species. At its core, the Universe is created as a place for growing souls.

Human religious traditions provide key concepts for understanding how the Universe and its advanced societies are "spiritual" and not merely "physical" in nature. You may ask if there is any fundamental difference between the spiritual and the material. Some say the spiritual world is actually more "real" than the material world. A Swedish physicist has reportedly even measured the weight of the human soul (about two ounces). It seems that the soul, a spiritual entity in most of Earth's traditions, coexists in the material world of the body. What we know as "spiritual" and "material" might just be other words for energy-life dimensions.

The User's Guide tells us that evolved dimensional beings, emanating from "spiritual" domains in the Universe, are permanently stationed around Earth, as part of the Universe society's presence. These beings carry out such functions as monitoring our life experiment planet and enforcing the quarantine. Although at times it may seem that the human events on our planet are chaotic, these dimensional spiritual beings are crucial to Earth's evolution, and ultimately to our re-integration into Universe society.

We humans are immersed in a very real spiritual-material ecology around Earth. This spiritual-material ecology, based on the twin energy principles of reflectivity and dimensionality, may be a key reason why we humans are not perceptually aware of the Universe society and its quarantine of Earth. Advanced civilizations can monitor us from afar through reflectivity, and can travel to Earth without being observed by us, by navigating through the Universe's multiple dimensions.

There is also a deeper reality to Universe society's enforcement of Earth's quarantine and its monitoring of Earth's evolution. More advanced civilizations within the Universe can be based in other "dimensions." Human religious traditions call these advanced dimensions "spiritual" or "Heavenly." The quarantine hypothesis suggests that these "Heavenly" domains are actual dimensions within the Universe that are different from the dimensions of time and space that we humans inhabit.

Our spiritual-material ecology makes it easy for a Universe society to communicate with an increasingly aware human population. Universe society has the technology to psychologically induce humanity into mass awareness of higher intelligent civilizations, through a mode of communication our psychology calls "peripheral cueing." Universe society uses a psychological reinforcement schedule to communicate subliminally with humans.

Covert human military-intelligence forces have also learned to mimic Universe society's communications. Their purpose is to fool us and thereby control our mass experience of what it means to be "extraterrestrial." At this stage of the planetary quarantine, there may still be negative organized extraterrestrial forces within Earth's dimensional ecology, operating outside of universal law.

A covert information war – carried out both by secret terrestrial power structures and by extraterrestrial forces themselves – has sharply polarized the human race about the existence of extraterrestrial visitors and the wisdom of integrating into Universe society. Some researchers hold that a hostile, colonizing extraterrestrial force is carrying out a secret genetic takeover of Earth, under the cover of psychological warfare and "alien abductions."

Other researchers hold that "alien abductions" are psychological warfare operations of a paramilitary nature, designed to sow confusion among humans about the extraterrestrial presence. The truth is that both sides – terrestrial and extraterrestrial – are engaged in an ongoing information war, with human attitudes as their target.

Exopolitics holds that all intelligent life in the Universe is subject to universal law, much as all human life on Earth is subject to what philosophers call "natural law." Exopolitics also holds the existence of a Universe-wide government. Thus, Extraterrestrial visitors to Earth are subject both to universal laws of justice, as well as the specific directives of a Universe government.

On Earth, a state of armed conflict may exist between certain governments; international gangs may carry out violent agendas; vandals may destroy the beauty of their urban targets. Yet international law and natural justice preserve our evolution.

It is the same situation with regard to Earth's position in the Universe. There may be extraterrestrial visitors who see our planet as an economic and genetic prize. Whatever their specific intentions may be, they are subject to universal law and to Universe government's ancient plans for this planet. We can best defend our position vis-à-vis these visitors through Exopolitics. We must become conscious that we live in a multi-party Universe, and that we can have the power of Universe law on our side.

11

The Information War and "Alien Abductions"

THE UFO PHENOMENON ITSELF can provide a psychological exit strategy from the effects of Earth's interplanetary quarantine. UFOs are a key to awakening humanity's awareness that Earth is part of a populated, advanced Universe society. It seems that many parties – both terrestrial and extraterrestrial alike – are competing for control of humanity's mass attention. The UFO phenomenon, however, is at the center of a secret information war that has raged continually among various terrestrial and extraterrestrial elements for the last 50 years.

An information war is a conflict of perceptions waged with the weapons of propaganda – misinformation, disinformation, and mind control. The strategic objective of the 50-year information war against Universe society has been to enforce total secrecy about the extraterrestrial presence in Earth's environment. When secrecy has failed, a secret terrestrial command-and-control network has resorted to misinformation, outright lies, and black propaganda about UFO sightings. Terrestrial commandos have also undertaken disinformation operations against the civilian population, such as the MILABs, the fake alien abductions staged by the military to portray the extraterrestrial presence as hostile or colonizing in nature.

Violence has also been used against individuals who attempt to break the information barrier. Mind control weapons are used to mentally disturb and economically destitute individuals who might break the extraterrestrial information embargo. Individuals have been threatened, tortured, and assassinated. The state terrorists who perpetrate such crimes feel safe in doing so because they operate under the cover of secrecy and the doctrine of plausible deniability.

The information war is the most acute reason why our reintegration with Universe society has not occurred yet. The principal aggressors in the anti-extraterrestrial information war appear to be military and intelligence authorities of the Anglo bloc, led by the United States, and including the United Kingdom, Canada, Australia, and New Zealand. These are the so-called "Echelon" countries, named after a secret surveillance system that they operate that intercepts all electronic communications worldwide and sorts them on a key word basis. The ultimate goal of this bloc is to deny humanity its universal heritage.

We must remember that the term "extraterrestrial" refers to organized Universe society, as it exists in interstellar and multi-dimensional space. Extraterrestrial societies are the participants in the exopolitical process. Exopolitics is a fundamental organizing, mediating, socializing, and governing process in interplanetary and inter-dimensional space. Exopolitics is how a highly populous and regulated Universe governs itself.

Despite the existence of such a regime, the information war is designed to sow confused, negative human attitudes about Extraterrestrial life. As we are discovering, our planet is still subject to many negative "alien" influences in the aftermath of the planetary quarantine. Universe quarantine refers to our disconnection from universal energy circuits, and from normal interaction with Universe society. We are still under the dominion and protection of Universe authorities.

The information war has as its goal the sowing of confusion about the extraterrestrial presence on Earth. The war's primary goal is to keep the existence of Universe society an official secret. Its secondary goal is to confound the world public about whether the extraterrestrial presence is benevolent or malevolent or a mixture of both – in order to demonize the extraterrestrial.

Universe society operates according to rules of law. Its intentions toward Earth are benign – we are its creatures. There are remnants of the planetary quarantine, however, which may operate within Earth's near environment. Some researchers maintain that alien abductions are part of a secret alien genetic plan to develop a "hybrid" intelligent species. This new species would replace the human race on Earth after its extinction in a coming ecological or near space catastrophe, such as an asteroid collision. Others hold that "rogue extraterrestrials" are secretly threatening Earth, but benevolent extraterrestrials will not let humanity be harmed.

As in all information wars premised upon secrecy, propaganda, and lies, it is difficult to know whether these information war scenarios are facts, distortions, or psychological projections. Some of the effects ascribed to "malevolent extraterrestrials" could in fact be products of the information war. These effects may in reality be the ploys of classic psychological warfare operations, and phenomena of the information war.

The "alien abduction" experiences that have been reported may be a mixture of other effects. They may be growth-oriented dimensional experiences of an archetypal nature. Abductions may be virtual or psychological operations by various sides in the information war, terrestrial and extraterrestrial alike. They can be disinformation MILABs, or terrestrial military-intelligence operations, mimicking "alien abductions" as part of the information war. Actual abduction by extraterrestrial forces may itself be a form of "psy war," or psychological warfare campaigns, against terrestrial military-intelligence networks. Alien abductions, in short, may not be what they seem at all.

The legacy of confusion from 50 years of information war has a practical antidote: the Decade of Contact. The information war must be ended and replaced by an education-based era of openness, public hearings, publicly funded research, and education about extraterrestrial reality.

There is some opinion, informed by scientific remote viewing, that it would be advantageous to humanity to enter into an open, voluntary, regulated genetic improvement program with at least one specific, spiritually advanced extraterrestrial race, the advanced Grays, for purposes of repairing the Grays' own genetic bank.[6] Such a regulated genetic program would not harm participating humans and would, on balance, be of great benefit to galactic society. The advanced Grays lost their home planet in the distant Universe past because of a self-induced ecological catastrophe, not unlike that which human society seems to be bringing upon itself on Earth. Some information indicates that these advanced Grays are now stockpiling genetic stocks of Earth flora and fauna, to facilitate our rebuilding of Earth at a future time. Universe networking and diplomatic relationship can help humanity mitigate impending ecological catastrophe that will befall Earth within several decades if we are unable to transform our fossil fuel civilization in time.

The principal lesson of Exopolitics appears to be that Universe politics is not anthropomorphic. We must be interactive members of Universe society with full rights, privileges, and duties. If we wish to protect our own exopolitical and genetic interests, for example, we must reach out to and integrate with Universe society. We must become participating members of the galactic family of planetary races.

12

Understanding
Universe Organization

IT IS NOT BY accident or delusion that between one-quarter and one-half of adult humans intuit that Earth has been visited by extraterrestrial civilizations. Viewing the whole of the Universe, the most logical and rational conclusion is that we live in a highly populous and organized Universe society of life-bearing planets. Like most basic decisions about reality, we can best arrive at this conclusion viscerally and intuitively.

Earth's dominant belief that the Universe is unpopulated is only as strong as the information upon which such a belief is based. The modern human belief that Earth is in a chaotic, sterile Universe is based on our own human projections. Using a common mechanism of psychological defense, projection, we project the supposition that advanced civilizations are like ours.

We also project that the Universe conforms to our human view of scientific laws. Our science and our imagination possess only the barest glimmerings of what advanced civilizations are like and what they know. The principles of reflectivity and dimensionality, for example, are officially unknown in our reality, although parascience gathers increasing knowledge of these principles.

What every intelligent life-bearing planetary society knows – that we are part of a highly organized Universe composed of billions of life-bearing planets – is treated as scientific heresy and madness in the establishment bastions of our planet. What is more, modern human society is unaware that we have been intentionally isolated through quarantine from interplanetary society.

The false illusion that we live in a lifeless Universe is, in effect, a conceptual artefact from past millennia when humanity thought that the Earth was itself the center of the Universe. This illusion, or mass delusion, is a lateral consequence of the Universe quarantine under which Earth has been labouring.

Were the planetary quarantine to be suddenly ended, we would have interplanetary commerce, transportation, communication, and participation. It is time for a fundamental re-assessment of what we know about the Universe in which we live. We are isolated Universe hermits only as a result of the delusional blinders put in place by the quarantine of Earth.

13

Universe Politics and
the Decade of Contact

THE END TO OUR planetary quarantine will be based on open interaction between Universe society and Earth. The teacher, Universe society, appears when the evolutionary student, Earth, is ready. The Universe is designed as a living environment for the education and evolution of consciousness. Our Universe isolation will end when we are ready for the next lesson. There is good reason to believe that the end of Earth's isolation in the Universe is now approaching.

We humans can reassess whether we live in a populated Universe simply by empowering ourselves to do so. Barring a massive overt demonstration on Earth by extraterrestrial society, we must make it socially and scientifically safe to reassess the issue of extraterrestrial civilizations in our environment.

Exopolitics is the best strategy to exit our planetary quarantine. As a central act of Exopolitics, let us create the Decade of Contact, a 10-year social program officially dedicated to examining the issues of extraterrestrial contact, a decade of official world participation in activating global consciousness and knowledge about Universe society.

Among the goals of the Decade of Contact would be the implementation of Exopolitics on Earth, the study of Earth's role in Universe government and politics. Through education, media, and grass roots politics, a Decade of Contact can bring awareness about Universe society to public consciousness, and can reorient human science and institutions to be "extraterrestrial friendly."

The transition from quarantine to open interaction with Universe society is the central aim of Exopolitics. Planetary reintegration requires active

Exopolitics in the form of Earth's participation in the politics of Universe society. This transition inevitably involves confronting the forces that consciously oppose the quarantine's end. Ignorance, pride, arrogance, jealousy, greed, and emptiness fuel Earth's covert hierarchy of power, which has waged an information war that has spanned the last 50 years. Exopolitics includes evolutionary forces that consciously favour integration with interplanetary society.

Ending the Universe quarantine of Earth is in some ways like any other political process, messy, with struggle between opposing forces. There are forces on Earth firmly committed to stopping a reunion with interplanetary civilization.

Those controlling the military, nuclear, and petroleum-based sectors of our civilization are firmly against a reunion with a Universe society that cannot be controlled. Access to the advanced propulsion systems of Universe society – namely "free or renewable energy" – would mean that the vested interests, embodied in private corporations and cartels, as well as the petroleum-based transportation and energy system that they control, would no longer be viable or even necessary.

Ultimately, breaking the quarantine would mean ending war and oppression. Human military establishments become obsolete as war is outlawed. The narrow human elite that perpetuates its power by maintaining the monopolies of petroleum production, nuclear power generation, and military weapons procurement would be deconstructed by interplanetary society.

Universe politics is the vehicle for our transformation into an interplanetary species of interstellar citizens. Crucial to exopolitical change is "mass awareness" on Earth. The polis, the human body politic, must become cognizant of its fundamental universal circumstances.

This change requires a critical mass of humans undergoing a changed perception of Universe in human society. A sea change in human attitudes about Earth is crucial to our re-integration into interplanetary society. Fundamentally, we must achieve a widespread understanding that we are part of a larger organized society in interstellar space.

Our attainment of a Universe relationship is vital to human reintegration with interstellar society. That is, we must deliberately enter into conscious relationships with the other civilizations of space and build on those relationships. These interrelationships with interplanetary society must be conscious and interactive, characterized by awareness, emotion, feeling, reciprocity, and mutual interest – all factors that we presently deny about intelligent life in outer space. We must dissolve our barriers of ignorance and cultural apathy about things not related to Earth.

Although we live in a highly populous Universe, we humans send but the barest feelers out towards space. Our dominant official attitude is a hardened belief that we are the only intelligent species and are entitled to carry our war-like, polluting, and dysfunctional ways out into the Universe. These are precisely the kinds of signals that the United States, through its militarization of space programs, is telegraphing to interplanetary society on our behalf.

14

Can We Heal?

AS WE REJOIN INTERPLANETARY society, our primary tasks will be to build a critical mass of human awareness and to develop interactive relationships with the rest of the intelligent Universe. These tasks call for profound human therapy, our own planetary healing.

Universal law may provide some consolation about our planetary need for healing. If interplanetary society quarantined us for good reason, then the quarantine is likely to be lifted only for equally good reason. Earth was put in quarantine not because we violated some law of astrophysics. We were quarantined from Universe society because Earth suffered a catastrophic violation of universal law. Therefore, Earth was subjected to interplanetary legal consequences. Natural law tells us that these consequences can be reversed. Reasonable grounds exist for the reversal of the quarantine and for allowing Earth to enter into knowing, conscious relationships with the rest of interplanetary society.

Human society has erected cultural barriers to understanding the true circumstances surrounding our place in the Universe. These cultural barriers cripple science and knowledge regarding issues of Universe society. Cultural barriers prevent formal education about Earth's period of isolation and planetary quarantine. As a planetary culture, we are in virtual ignorance about our fundamental condition in the Universe. The future now lies in our hands. You may be ready as an individual, but we must ready humanity as a whole for Universe society.

Historically, we humans have been unable to openly acknowledge the existence of Universe society. In retrospect, the Universe quarantine has been successful. Our collective heads remain in a cosmic paper bag, and we have not been able to find our way out. After all, the plot of Earth's history as a wayward planet is as plausible as any science fiction thriller about good and evil in the Universe.

A Decade of Contact can create our collective breakthrough into interplanetary society. The most logical and intuitive insight is that the Universe is populated and organized. The Decade of Contact takes this life-affirming insight and gives it positive social reinforcement.

The Decade of Contact deconstructs the barriers between Universe society and human science, education, communication, government, community politics, and religion. During the decade, we will rekindle our collective human desire to experience the unity of the Universe. The Decade of Contact reaffirms Universe integration as a most profound duty of human governments, religious and educational institutions, and families.

15

An End to
Permanent Warfare

IN UNIVERSE SOCIETY, LOVE, rather than conflict, is the central organizing principle among advanced civilizations. A heritage of our planetary quarantine is that military aggression, political oppression, and economic exploitation are the predominant means of self-government. Our conflict-based human civilization persists because of our enforced isolation. We have come to accept conflict, oppression, and suffering as normal. Earth's culture of conflict is an aberration in the Universe. Earthly conflict will fall away with our admission into Universe society.

Earth's enslavement to a permanent warfare economy and to a military, petroleum, and nuclear-based network of power elites will end upon our open integration into Universe society. With access to the advanced technologies of Universe society, Earth will no longer be dependent on an energy infrastructure that is environmentally degrading. Earth's energy infrastructure is owned by a narrow, terrestrially oriented oligarchy, which actively resists Universe society.

One of the benefits of Earth's integration into Universe society is that the military-industrial complex that US President Dwight D. Eisenhower (1890-1969) warned us about will no longer devour an overwhelming share of Earth's gross product. Earth's unaccountable system of corrupt, violent governments will be transformed into more universal forms. The educational, religious, and cultural establishments of Earth, which hold blinders of ignorance over the collective human mind, likewise will be transformed upon our integration into Universe society.

In short, our planetary civilization will enter an unprecedented era of development for humanity on Earth. Unparalleled democratization and expansion of individual liberties will accompany our integration into Universe society. The permanent warfare economy will be transformed into a sustainable, cooperative Space Age society, one integrated with a larger Universe society.

The permanent warfare economy and a network of reigning oligarchies and secret agencies work to keep humanity divided and ignorant of its Universe heritage. This network's intent has been to prevent advanced Universe technologies they do not own from transforming our way of life and standard of living. The permanent warfare economy controls Earth's politics and resources, and strives to delay humanity's re-integration into interstellar society for as long as possible.

As cited above, the richest 250 individuals or families retain more of the Earth's wealth than do the 2.5 billion poorest persons. Restated, the wealthiest 250 persons or families own more than half of the entire human race. There is something fundamentally rotten about this equation. A malevolent spirit of avarice animates human plutocratic elites on Earth. This gross inequality will end when the global economy becomes part of the galactic one, and humanity adopts the energy systems and cost accounting methods of the Universe.

The information war perpetuates and enhances the effects of our quarantine from Universe society by keeping humanity ignorant and isolated from the rest of Universe society. The permanent warfare economy and its networks of command and control play a dysfunctional role similar to the catastrophic one that led to the imposition of our planetary quarantine in the first place. Perhaps this fossil fuel-nuclear civilization consciously intends to impede humanity's universal destiny. The power structure's hidden objective may be to delay our planetary progress as conscious beings and trans-temporal souls. We humans must demand the right to open reunion with our fellow Universe civilizations.

It is difficult to predict the full consequences of the reunion of Earth with interstellar civilization. We have no recent experience of open interaction with evolved civilizations. We can surmise that other planets have been placed in isolation. There is a regular, staged process of reintegrating planets into open participation with Universe society. Indeed, Earth may be embarking upon a path that has been tread before in the Universe.

We have experienced centuries and millennia of flawed social programming in Earth society. If you want to grasp that the Universe is actually highly populous and organized, then activate your spirit of the contrary. Contraire spirit leads one to turn dogma upside down, and to look beyond the accepted canon of misinformation. Our complacency builds castles of cosmic misinformation in our collective human mind: Yes, the Earth is the center of the Universe. Yes, the Earth is the only populated planet. Yes, only fools believe that extraterrestrial civilizations know about Earth and visit it.

In reality, only the under-informed believe the Universe is unpopulated. Not much has changed in the *modus operandi* of the oligarchy enforcing Earthly ignorance over the last several thousand years. Our dominant political culture – violent, conflict-prone, and terrestrially blinded – is like a dangerous obsessive abuser. Human political culture would rather keep humanity in the bondage of ignorance than allow the human race to advance to its next evolutionary destination.

Like any abusive relationship, our relationship to the dominant terrestrial civilization can be changed. We can leave behind our imprisoning terrestrial culture and transport ourselves into our real interstellar selves. We can affirm, as individuals and as a global body politic, that we are citizens of the Universe. By changing our own consciousness, we can let go of the abusive programming that isolation has foisted on us. Eventually, our new consciousness can grow into the mass mind of human Universe citizens. Humanity will join Universe society through a dedicated Decade of Contact.

16

Reversing the Quarantine

AN OLD ADAGE SAYS, "The world will always be with us." Well, it is humanity's exopolitical ignorance that keeps our world isolated and unaware. We can move beyond our collective ignorance. We must navigate our way out of isolation from the rest of Universe society. Our ability to devise a path out of ignorance is a test as to whether we are ready to be released from this planetary quarantine.

Human science and technology are primed to discover that the Universe is organized around life-bearing planets. One key step in human science's ability to discover planetary society occurred on November 5th, 1999. Scientists at the University of California at Berkeley detected a planet near star HD 209458, in the constellation Pegasus, about 153 million light years (a million billion miles) from Earth. Astronomer Geoffrey Marcy stated that the planet, observable through its eclipse with its sun, gave humanity its first independent scientific confirmation of a non-local planet. A few weeks later, on November 22nd, 1999, British scientists at St. Andrew's University in Scotland reported isolating the light from a planet orbiting the star Tau Bootes, about 50 light years from Earth.

With the ability to detect planets, human science achieved a milestone in creating building blocks to an early interplanetary understanding. In fact, since 1993, Earth astronomers have discovered 28 extra-solar planets. Five of the six planets discovered in 1999 are in the "habitable zone." This means that their environments can support liquid water, which is a prerequisite for life. The goal of the scientists at St. Andrew's is to discover solar systems that have Earth-like, life-bearing planets.

This newfound ability of science to detect life-bearing planets seems synchronistic, coming, as it does, just as we are being prepared to leave behind our planetary quarantine. Advanced evolutionary laws guide Earth in its re-integration with Universe society. We are in a collective illusion, one that makes it seem that we are alone in a Universe devoid of other intelligent life. In fact, not only are we not alone, we are guided in each step along our journey back into cosmic society.

The integration of intelligent life-bearing planets into Universe society follows a staged progression. Life-bearing planets such as Earth are constantly monitored by interplanetary society. The state of our planetary civilization – from our science to our wars – is played back in real-time to interplanetary society. It is within our power to secure our release from enforced isolation by transforming and fine-tuning how we behave as a planet. We can dramatically improve our quality of life by becoming openly aware that the rest of interplanetary society is monitoring us.

It is a genuine mistake to think that we are alone in our planetary destiny. No matter how long the Universe reintegration process takes, even millennia, we are guided by higher intelligences at multiple levels. Our imprisoned culture may not allow us to express or feel this Universe guidance openly. Human culture will change as we expand into the Universe and into new dimensions of parascience and evolving consciousness.

Soon, it will no longer be considered taboo for a scientist to work openly on the task of reintegrating Earth into Universe society. We will be guided in our planetary evolution by our own nature as interstellar and inter-dimensional beings.

Advanced extraterrestrial, extra-dimensional civilizations are here to help us grow into new governmental, political, and social forms. Just because our culture does not acknowledge their presence does not mean that they do not exist. Spiritual dimensions are as real as the material dimensions of time and space with which we are so familiar.

Multi-dimensional "spiritual" beings guide us in our planetary development. Our Universe is fundamentally a spiritual experience, and the material world is but one platform within reality. The spiritual dimensions of the Universe guide us outward into the reaches of interplanetary space and inward into the reaches of the human soul.

We humans are interstellar beings with the potential of becoming a functioning interplanetary civilization. In this evolutionary task, we are guided by more advanced multi-dimensional civilizations. Officially, our human culture does not now acknowledge these higher civilizations.

Nevertheless, the civilizations are there, and they communicate to us symbolically in the face of a hostile human authority. Their intent is not to overwhelm us, which they could easily do.

Higher civilizations intend to heal us from the mass delusion of separateness from the rest of intelligent creation. We can make friends with these advanced forces of the Universe by allowing our unconscious and higher selves to accept their presence. A growing conscious relationship among humans and multi-dimensional Universe forces is part of Earth's ongoing spiritual revolution. Nurturing our relationships with Universe forces is part of reintegrating Earth with the rest of the Universe.

One way to strengthen your direct connection with the intelligent Universe is by cultivating awareness of cosmic patterns. Contemplating the patterns of Earth's connections with the Cosmos can help bond you with a larger Universe society. Were you to live on a non-quarantined planet, the interconnectedness of intelligent life in the Universe would be more apparent. As it is, on Earth, our cosmic connections are hidden, visible only to "eyes that see" and "ears that hear."

Earth grows souls that are extraordinarily hardy, and are highly regarded throughout the Universe. We grow a unique species of intelligent souls on Earth, souls that can live on hope alone. We humans possess extraordinary inner strength, the strength of the human soul. Once we are made conscious of our isolation from Universe, we will have the strength to move ourselves out of the cosmic bubble we are in. We will come to understand the scientific, historical, physical, emotional, mental, and spiritual aspects of our Earthly quarantine, and move collectively to end it.

Fear is a dominant emotion that still governs human civilization. Fear is a remnant of the planetary cataclysmic rebellion and subsequent quarantine. Humans fear that one nation will attack another, that disease will destroy us, that we will be economically deprived, that we will fall behind our competitors, that our children will suffer. Fear is regressive, the dominant emotion that keeps us in ignorance of our Universe heritage and consigns us to quarantine. Fear paralyses us as a civilization, leaving us locked in global and personal insecurity. The familiar nostrum that "we have nothing to fear but fear itself" is a deep cosmic truth.

Rejoining interstellar civilization is our evolutionary heritage. We are destined for Universe citizenship because we are interstellar, dimensional beings with trans-temporal souls. Our own collective consciousness can either speed up or slow down our journey towards Universe society. If we insist on remaining enmeshed in planetary melodrama, we will remain quarantined as we are now. We have reached a key evolutionary moment, as we perceive our planetary history and our future as an interplanetary species. There is no logical reason for stalling any longer. We can structure a systematic program to help Earth rejoin Universe society.

A powerful barrier keeping us locked within a terrestrial isolation is our Earth-bound culture. Our imprisoned culture repeats its patterns of waging wars, building military establishments, supporting tyrannies, weaponizing outer space, oppressing populations, committing genocide, and engaging in mass mind control of humanity. Our culture is now hijacked by elites, that maintain this destructive agenda and deny Earth its Universe citizenship.

From the perspective of those who monitor Earth on behalf of Universe society, there is a moral bottom line to our collective behaviour on Earth. What keep us imprisoned in quarantine are the violent, regressive patterns of our war-like society. In the eyes of Universe society, war and ecocide have negative consequences for human civilization. Perpetual warfare and ecological degradation of the planet mark us as a backward civilization incapable of participating in the advanced Universe scheme of things.

Earth's behavioural transformation cannot happen overnight. A massive demonstration of Universe society's presence would defeat an important purpose of our planetary quarantine. The path out of quarantine is interactive. The more we openly interact with Universe society, the less the quarantine.

17

Reaching Out to
Interstellar Society

THE SEARCH FOR EXTRATERRESTRIAL Intelligence (SETI) program could be an important interactive step in reaching out to join interstellar society. But SETI has its conceptual limitations. Universe society knows full well that Earth is populated. The deliberate isolation of our planet is understood and enforced throughout the Universe.

But SETI's very existence is a plus for Earth. SETI proves that humanity is at a developmental stage where it can acknowledge interaction with other intelligent civilizations. SETI embodies our first institutional steps to reach out to fellow civilizations in the Universe. These civilizations already know, of course, that we are in enforced isolation. SETI's true significance is that humanity can exhibit rational social behaviour in outer space.

Programs like SETI are a starting point for interactive Exopolitics. To search for extraterrestrial intelligence, we must first acknowledge Earth as a quarantined planet in an interstellar society. In order to achieve open contact with intelligent extraterrestrial civilizations, a complete transformation of SETI's conceptual framework must occur.

Scientists Frank Drake and the late Carl Sagan founded SETI in the 1960s. SETI's concept of the Universe is in some sense founded on the famous Drake Equation. This equation, as set out by Frank Drake and SETI, is:

$$N = R* \ fp \ ne \ fl \ fi \ fc \ L$$

N is said to equal the total number of intelligent, communicating civilizations in our galaxy, the Milky Way. According to Drake, these are those "whose electromagnetic signals and/or emissions are detectible." As "N" turns out to be a relatively large number, it is this equation that is thought to justify the search for extraterrestrial intelligence.

Drake hesitates to estimate precisely how many civilizations there are in the Milky Way galaxy. In arriving at the total number of planets with intelligent, communicating civilizations on them in the Milky Way galaxy, he lists the following factors in his now-famous Drake equation: (R*) the Rate of formation of stars suitable for development of intelligent civilization; (fp) the fraction of the R* stars which have planets; (ne) the number of planets in each such (fp) solar system that are suitable for life; (fl) the fraction of these (ne) planets on which life actually develops; (fi) the fraction of these (fl) life-bearing planets on which intelligent life develops; (fc) the fraction of planets with intelligent life on which a technological civilization develops and releases signals of its existence into space; and (L) the length of time these intelligent civilizations release such signals into space.

Drake himself admits that the result of this equation is highly problematical. The entire formula is based on only one sample – that of the intelligent civilization of Earth. Thus, the result is apt to be either a human projection of evolution on Earth, or a total speculation about evolution elsewhere in the Universe. There are no factors in the equation on which SETI is based that reflect the true and practical determinants of human communication with Universe civilizations. The Drake equation and the present SETI program do not contain a factor which states "Earth in quarantine; communication not permitted."

SETI can search galaxy after galaxy for signals from extraterrestrial civilizations, without apparent response, and conclude its efforts have gone unrecognized by intelligent civilizations. Yet nothing could be further from the truth. SETI is not fundamentally flawed; it is just incomplete in terms of its approach. Interstellar civilizations are busy monitoring us to see whether the conditions for response and dialogue have been met.

SETI's task is not just scientific communication. Rather, its true task is exopolitical. How do we humans present ourselves where higher intelligence would want to communicate? How do we begin the dialogue to end the quarantine and resume an open membership in interplanetary society?

Exopolitics can provide a solution to the dilemma of those like Dr. Hal Puthoff and his colleagues, as well as Washington, D.C.'s Brookings Institute, who believe that "despite the UFO phenomenon having continued now for over two generations, the huge technological head start of the [extraterrestrials] would come as a shock to many scientists as well as citizenry... It would be so great as to seriously challenge our consensual reality, a not insignificant danger."[7]

Exopolitics provides the conceptual bridge between the terrestrial consensual reality and the consensual reality of Universe society. An exopolitical relationship between terrestrial society and Universe society is the process by which our consensual reality can integrate and normalize with that of a more advanced off-planet culture, so that cultural shock becomes cultural integration and mutuality of attraction between terrestrial and extraterrestrial civilizations. With Exopolitics there is not shock, but relationship and meaningful interaction.

18

The Rebirth of
Universal Consciousness

"AS ABOVE, SO BELOW" is one principle by which Earth facilitates its Universe reunion. Earth can consciously connect to advanced interplanetary society (above), and mirror this cosmic principle here on Earth (below). Through open interaction with Universe society, we humans can transform Earth into a free, non-quarantined planet. There is no better way we could spend our time on Earth.

As individuals, we may not have to do anything as part of our reunion with Universe society. Universe consciousness is part of the growth of personal intuition among a large percentage of the human population. The remarkable increase in intuitive awareness of an extraterrestrial presence on Earth is a good example. Whatever the motivating force, the human population is becoming aware of Universe civilizations on Earth.

Major human governments are hostile to any extraterrestrial initiative toward Earth. Academia and the "knowledge" establishments have likewise been aggressively hostile toward an extraterrestrial role in our planetary affairs. A covert military-intelligence establishment seems to be running disinformation-based extraterrestrial masquerade programs with the intent of "owning" the extraterrestrial experience. Yet these transparent frauds do not dilute the intuitive human experience that genuine extraterrestrial civilizations exist.

Subliminal communication is one important source for increasing human awareness of extraterrestrial activities around Earth. Universe civilizations are communicating with humans subliminally and at the level of peripheral awareness. This peripheral cueing forms a stage in Universe society's overall strategy to integrate humanity into open interplanetary society. Through subliminal awareness, a critical mass of humanity is becoming consciously connected to the organized Cosmos.

Advanced Universe psychologists gently work to trigger a cognitively retarded human species into full Universe consciousness, without overwhelming them with fear or paralysis. Up to 45 percent of Earth's most affluent and educated human adults may have become Universe conscious through extraterrestrial subliminal programs. If so, this is an extraordinary success rate, one that bodes well for our full Universe reintegration.

Universal law governs humanity's ascent into full Universe consciousness. Earth's evolution differs from that of a normal evolving life-bearing planet in that we are in quarantine from interplanetary society. On normal life-bearing planets, open participation in Universe society starts at the very beginnings of planetary civilization. From the point-of-view of Universe society, Earth is unique among intelligent civilizations.

We humans are now beginning open Universe integration. This is a process that occurs according to evolutionary laws governing advanced civilization. That we are ignorant of Universe laws does not make us any the less subject to them. We are an entry-level intelligent species becoming aware of the society of intelligent species in the larger Universe.

A critical mass, open to union with interstellar society, is gathering. The truth is that we are on a path to rejoin a greater society. As individuals, we can choose to experience this process as a positive opportunity, or we can resist and regress.

Fear and ignorance fuels most of the resistance to Universe integration. Humanity's open integration into the organized Universe is for our long-term benefit. Our evolutionary cycle at this stage offers opportunities, providing we interact positively with Universe society. Of course, we can choose self-destructive reaction to Universe society's approach and plan. Even that would be but a temporary setback in Earth's inevitable integration into interstellar society.

Humanity is at a stage analogous to when we were first entering the Universe quarantine, only now, instead of being isolated from the organized Universe, we are rejoining Universe society. Our reintegration is made possible by our universal awareness. Exopolitics provides a conceptual structure that will allow Earth's Universe re-integration to take place. Major planetary transformation can occur within the framework of Exopolitics.

Official science denies there is organized advanced life that is actively involved with Earth. In order to control public opinion's psychological gateways to Universe reintegration, secret disinformation ploys about Universe society by military and intelligence agencies mimic "extraterrestrial activity." Covertly orchestrated confusion feeds human attitudes and knowledge about extraterrestrial intelligence. Science fiction literature and cinema may paint a dark future for humanity in outer space. Each of these visions seems to be founded on fear, ignorance, or error, and to advance the agenda of powerful vested interests.

Compare these false, negative portrayals of the Universe with our intuitive knowledge that the Universe is organized and benign. A positive vision of life in an organized Universe is extravagant and blissful. It is not dark, fearful, conflict-ridden, or slave-like. The oligarchy that controls our terrestrial petroleum-nuclear civilization is opposed to reunion with Universe society. Our military, petroleum, and nuclear establishments may likely deconstruct when the dimensional "free energy" of advanced Universe society becomes the technological norm on Earth.

Advanced interplanetary society does not allow war. Planetary evolution on Earth will mean an end to human war as a means of production, wealth creation, or social oppression. Universe society spells the demise of militarism on Earth and in our near space environment.

Reunion with Universe civilizations will bring a closer relationship with God. The most advanced scientific reality in all creation is that God is source. As our relationship with the Universe expands, religious institutions must adapt as humanity learns that many of the details of their belief system may be mythical and scientifically false. As Earth becomes part of interplanetary society, humanity will finally cease to war against itself in the name of God.

Terrestrial power and war-making structures will largely deconstruct in the Universe reunion. Earth's officially enforced ignorance about Universe society is no accident. You have not heard much about the organized Universe because there are powerful forces opposed to our union with Universe society. Information about Universe society has been kept from us to ensure the *status quo* for a narrow human ownership class that is wedded to the past.

Universe politics – Exopolitics – empowers us in our goal of reunion. We can join Universe politics by establishing open public venues for Exopolitics. Public, community-based venues can provide the political tools to decide how public and private resources will be used in our integration with Universe society. A Universe reunion will involve a commitment of our entire civilization, planet, collective future, and way of life.

It is time that we humans play the game of Universe politics openly and collectively. Understandably, you may feel disempowered or disenfranchised on Universe issues. There is no more important human question than whether we join this greater society, and its advanced government, civilizations, technologies, and peoples. As an individual, you will want to have input into whether your planet rejoins interstellar society. In Universe politics, all movement is inevitably forward and ultimately to our collective benefit. Even momentary adversity and upset in the process of reintegration into the organized Universe can bring its own benefits.

The essence of Universe politics is simple: we humans are not alone; we are in a collective Universe society. As a species, we do not have ultimate title to and possession of our planet and interplanetary space. Earth is a universal commons. We exist in the Universe subject to Universe laws. We are in a multi-party Universe, on a multi-party planet.

As we embark on the process of mobilizing our human awareness, we will find that we have the help and resources of a very advanced civilization that is organized throughout universal space. Universe politics is how we humans relate to Universe society; how we enforce our rights in organized interplanetary society; how we request and seek out Universe society's resources and responsibilities for our planet.

19

Toward a Decade of Contact

FEAR SHOULD NO LONGER paralyse us from seeking out membership in Universe society. One version of this fear, promoted by the military and intelligence establishment, is that we should fear an "invasion" of hostile aliens more than anything else.

Contemporary world leaders have said that such a hostile invasion would truly bring humanity together. A US president broadcast this message to the world in the early 1980s at the UN, as did another as recently as 1999. In a way, this "alien invasion" mindset is the modern equivalent of the "Earth is the center of the Universe" worldview of the ignorant and superstitious Middle Ages.

The "alien invasion" scenario is a psychological warfare initiative. It is but one more way that powerful terrestrial governments with vested interests keep the human population isolated from the advances of interplanetary civilization. What will bring humanity together is our accessing interplanetary government. There is no authentic "alien invasion" planned. That is disinformation. Universe government is advanced, organized, peaceful, and interested in our evolution. If there is any "rogue" extraterrestrial presence on Earth, it operates outside the confines of Universe laws and will end.

How can the human population get beyond the anti-extraterrestrial conceptual traps that our institutions and terrestrial leaders keep constructing for us? One way is to build a new, participatory exopolitical process the purpose of which is to foment and structure humanity's preparedness to enter interplanetary society. Exopolitics will deconstruct negative disinformation about an extraterrestrial presence. Open research will shed the light of truth on alleged extraterrestrial plots to genetically enslave the human race.

The Decade óf Contact is a 10-year participatory education-based process to facilitate integration with Universe society. We dedicate a 10-year period of education and community action around integrating Earth into Universe society. The Decade of Contact is both a process and a public attitude. Extraterrestrial contact is our doorway into re-integration with Universe society. Extraterrestrial contact is an interactive process; it involves mutual interaction between our fellow humans and Universe society. Just how many decades it will take to re-establish working contact with the organized Universe is partially in our own hands.

The Decade of Contact is simple and straightforward. Any individual, group, institution, nation, or government can participate. Participants in the Decade of Contact will commit to transform their lives, institutional focus, and resources to re-establishing integration with organized interplanetary society. Rejoining Universe society is an exopolitical process, and will happen only as political momentum gathers at the personal, local, regional, and global levels. The process of Universe integration may take time during lift-off, like a space vehicle starting its long journey with a slow ascent from Earth.

Mobilizing the human species to integrate with Universe society will take place in many concurrent ways. A key task is the gathering of information, research, and scientific and educational resources about Universe society. Our dominant terrestrial model of reality is functionally a legacy from the Middle Ages. Our collective new knowledge base must be assembled from an exopolitical context.

There are also important cultural components to the Decade of Contact, as human awareness builds to a critical mass. These will include political movements, public events, musical concerts, art exhibits, and media productions to celebrate Universe society. Our reunion with Universe society is a ground of our basic human rights. The Decade of Contact process will transform our civilization from within, from a terrestrial culture to a universal one.

Transformation of human society will occur when we reach a Universe-sensitive critical mass. With approximately 45 percent of Earth's population now extraterrestrial-conscious, can a critical mass be far behind?

20

The End of
Terrestrial Politics?

THERE ARE MANY CYCLES in Earth's Exopolitics. We are building on the spiral of a long planetary history. We are winning back our Universe citizenship, lost eons ago and intentionally kept hidden from us over the years by terrestrial governments and power-greedy groups. Now, all that is about to be transformed.

In 1977, a US presidential administration was open enough to acknowledge its ignorance about a wider universal reality in our midst. The highest democratically elected authority in the United States sought the most creative of our sciences to understand the open approaches of Universe society. But an anti-Universe information war intervened to scuttle a Carter White House study of extraterrestrial communication. That was one of my first personal experiences with the devastating effects of the information war.

Our Exopolitics is also part of other, longer cycles. Historically, the fundamental rights of humanity, hard-won in political struggle and revolutions against old repressive orders of reality, are part of our exopolitical development. In ages past, Earth was once a member of an interplanetary society. Each one of you will decide whether this possibility is worthy of your consideration.

Exopolitics brings us into our collective Universe bodies politic. Politics is a process of mediating among various interests within a larger framework. Politics is more than an academic, analytic exercise. Politics is about the freedom of our bodies from want and of our minds from fear. Politics is about mutual empowerment, and our universal heritage is the ultimate empowerment in our known reality.

A narrowly focused military-intelligence-plutocratic power elite attempts to lead our entire generation of Earthlings into believing a planetary lie – that we are alone in the Universe. But we are not alone.

The political process and governmental structures we have on Earth do not stop at Earth's geo-stationary orbit. Politics, government, and individual freedom extend throughout the interstellar and inter-dimensional Universe that we inhabit. Government on Earth is derived from exo-government in the Universe, and we all have inalienable rights in the Universe.

We know that the era of terrestrial politics is over, and a new age is beginning. The age of Universe politics has now landed. How this new exopolitical age will unfold – whether violently and repressively or expansively and freely – is in some sense up to each of us. We are a nucleus of politically sensitive terrestrials that are aware that the playing field is vast. We are part of a new dimension of Universe government as it dawns on Earth.

Remember, secret networks in some terrestrial governments continue to keep the people in the dark about Universe government and Universe politics. Look to your own government in the United States or one of the other Anglo-bloc countries – Britain, Canada, Australia, and New Zealand. This group carries on a secret information war against our right to Universe participation. These are the same governments that manage the global surveillance network Echelon. [8] The Echelon governments seem to have the largest participation in waging the anti-Universe information war.

In contrast, unofficial governmental networks, like those in France, seem to be open to the extraterrestrial presence. COMETA, a three-year study by former French space and air force officials, validated an extraterrestrial presence around Earth. [9]

The Echelon countries, led by the United States, continue this anti-Universe war for global power and global wealth. Echelon hides a secret government network that exists to protect a global petroleum-nuclear civilization, a military-industrial complex. Its military and intelligence agency-based command and control system is a private army. The anti-Universe war is a private war prosecuted to prevent an era of free energy and expansive Universe citizenship from dawning on Earth. This oligarchy is attempting to own the future and keep us in an oppressive past.

Every citizen of Earth is a victim of the information war against Universe integration. This interplanetary war exists in order to perpetuate the concentration of wealth and justify the mind control technology of a narrow, brutal, retrogressive elite. Some of us have suffered more directly at their hands than have others. Our entire planetary reality suffers war, poverty, disease, crime, and environmental degradation (including species extinction), all legitimized by a pervasive ethic of selfishness.

The very knowledge that we are part of an organized, interstellar, multi-dimensional society makes our new Universe citizenship a reality. Knowledge itself will begin to evaporate the power of our selfish and destructive civilization. Our so-called terrestrial power structure will no longer be big fish in a small pond, but micro-personalities in an infinite ocean of reality, the Universe itself.

Exopolitics' essential message is that we, the human population, are all collectively the exo-government, the planetary Universe society. In the United States alone, between 50 and 100 hundred million adult residents are aware that Universe society visits Earth. Seventy percent of the US population disbelieves the official government information war. In other countries where governmental mass mind control is not as great, such as Brazil, even larger percentages of the population know that we are Universe citizens.

Terrestrial government is a hollow shell game, an atavistic remnant of the planetary rebellion. The evaporation of terrestrial government and the birthing of Universe government are inevitable. There is no "take me to your leader" scenario in our future. The entire Cosmos knows that the leaders of the Earth's information war are corrupt and unworthy to lead us further. All they value is profit and control.

We, the human population, can all help land a new universal reality and Universe society into our terrestrial dimension from the inside. Our own inner awareness can shift its allegiance from terrestrial-based reality to a Universe-based reality. In such a paradigm, war and ignorance are no longer acceptable problem-solving alternatives. There are many tactical and strategic roadways Exopolitics can take over the coming years. It would be best that they be taken in a common Decade of Contact.

In the late 1970s, the US White House under President Jimmy Carter anticipated the later study by France's COMETA validating extraterrestrials in our environment. That prophetic effort was brutally terminated by the information war, using the mind control technology of the military.[10] Exopolitics now cycles back again, this time to prevail.

Let us set aside a special Decade of Contact to assimilate extraterrestrial contact. In all countries, let us push for legislative hearings, scientific and policy studies, community politics, and exopolitical process. There is no doubt that our present terrestrial fabric – educational, constitutional, scientific, entertainment – needs to be transformed as part of a new Universe-based reality.

PART FOUR

From Star Wars to Star Dreams

HOW IT IS WITHIN humanity's scientific and exopolitical capability to integrate with off-planet cultures for mutual benefit, through programs of public interest diplomacy with those cultures now visiting Planet Earth.

Integrating with
Off-Planet Cultures (OPCs)

HUMANITY HAS THE SCIENTIFIC and exopolitical tools with which to integrate with off-planet cultures (OPCs). One task of the Decade of Contact is to develop public interest diplomacy for outreach and integration with a possible off-planet culture on Mars and other willing, spiritually evolved off-planet cultures now visiting Earth.

Scientific Remote Viewing (SRV)

Scientific remote viewing is the trained psychic ability to access information from any geographic location or being whether that location or being is located in a past, present, or future timeframe.[11] Scientific remote viewing enables two-way interactive communications between telepathic beings that may be in different physical or dimensional locations in the Universe, as well as in different timeframes. For example, scientific remote viewing interactive communications may take place between a human researcher, located in a laboratory in Atlanta, Georgia in the mid-1990s, and members of the galactic federation central council, located in another dimension of the galaxy. These communications may address the nature of galactic governance and other key exopolitical issues.

Scientific remote viewing trials are accomplished through a scientific methodology in which the viewer does not know what he or she will view or communicate with in advance. Remote viewing research was carried out by Dr. Hal Puthoff and Russell Targ at Stanford Research Institute (SRI) in the 1970s and further developed by the CIA and the US military in the 1980s. It became a stunningly accurate intelligence data collection tool before becoming partially declassified in the mid-1990s.[12]

Through scientific remote viewing, key researchers in the area of exopolitical relations between human and off-planet cultures have identified key characteristics and goals of an apparent off-planet culture on Mars.[13] This present-day Martian off-planet culture, humanoid in form, lives under the surface of Mars, as well as on Earth in underground bases in the United States of America, and in intentional rural colonies in South America.

This Martian culture reportedly may be survivors of a Martian-solar system cataclysm in the distant past. The survivors of the Martian culture were rescued from this past cataclysm in a time travel operation approved by a galactic governing body known as the "galactic federation." The time travel rescue operation was reportedly conducted by an off-planet culture known as the "Advanced Grays."

The surviving Martian culture, now existing under the surface of present-day Mars, is about 150 years in advance technologically of our present-day human civilization. The scientific remote viewing data suggest that the Martian off-planet culture may wish to initiate contact and integration with human civilization, including migration to Earth, as living conditions on Mars are difficult for the long-term. These initial data suggest that mutual benefits to the Martian off-planet culture and to our human civilization might result from good will contact and public interest diplomacy between our two cultures, and set out a proposed general course of action for mutual contact.

A public interest diplomacy initiative undertaken by human society would confirm if these data generated by scientific remote viewing are accurate in stating that there is intelligent life on Mars today as described, and if Martian society desires to integrate with human civilization at this time for purposes of mutual aid.

The public release of scientific remote viewing data that Mars was once a planet that was hospitable to life and still hosts life today was met with scientific skepticism when first published in 1996. Though many people dismiss it as a coincidence, what has stunned some skeptics is that since the publication of this scientific remote viewing finding, the following information is now generally accepted to be factual:

- Mars once had saltwater oceans;

- Microbial life once existed on Mars, as evidenced by a Mars meteor that has impacted Earth;

- Both methane and ammonia have been discovered in the current Martian atmosphere. Science demonstrates that such gases can only result from current life or from recent volcanic activity, the latter of which has not been found;

- More and more scientists, such as Mars specialist Gilbert Levin, admit that life on Mars today is likely. [14]

The Star Dreams Initiative (SDI)

We can call the public interest diplomacy outreach program to off-planet cultures, like the surviving one on Mars, a "Star Dreams Initiative (SDI)." Star Dreams can offer an alternate vision to the weaponization of space, or Star Wars.

Star Wars represents our continued obsession with war, by exporting the permanent warfare economy, space-based weapons, and active warfare into outer space. Star Wars is a choice that involves going with the internal emotions of fear, aggression, conflict, non-trust, control over others, and a desire to move towards a future of perpetual war, agony, and suffering. This choice leads to a nightmare on Earth.

Star Dreams represents a transformation of our war industry into a peaceful, cooperative, sustainable Space Age society, and integrating with an intelligent, organized Universe society. The choice of peace is a choice that almost every man, woman, and child can dream of. Star Dreams embraces the ideals of caring about life, curiosity, exploration, trust, cooperation and a desire to move towards a more spiritual future. Supporting initiatives, such as an international UN Space Preservation Treaty to ban space-based weapons and warfare in space, is a legal step towards Star Dreams. The Star Dreams choice leads to hope for our future.

Choosing Star Dreams and banning war in space and space-based weapons will lead to the transformation of the permanent war economy into a peaceful and global cooperative space exploration society. We will then create a system of communication and cooperation with technologically and spiritually advanced off-planet cultures that are presently engaging our world. Such cooperation will potentially lead to helping resolve some of our coming environmental problems on Earth.

The universal paradigm of a Star Dreams Initiative will help increase cooperation on Earth. It will gradually be used to help create more unity in the worldviews of national and international decision-makers, as well as our human cultures, religions, military, corporations, organizations, media, communities, families, and individuals.

A Star Dreams Initiative (SDI) will be inspiring, compelling, and beneficial for all of humanity, as we work together to make the best of our situation on Earth. We are at a pivotal point in our history and have the opportunity as at no other time in human history. We can collectively imagine what we want the next 50 years of humanity to be like and we can choose the shining spiritual legacy of Star Dreams.

The Exopolitics Model and Science

The essential structure and dynamics of the Exopolitics Model – that the Universe is populated by intelligent civilizations, organized under governing bodies and operating according to law – is preliminarily confirmed by replicable scientific remote viewing data developed during the 1990s. Data from scientific remote viewers suggest that a spiritually and technologically advanced galactic federation of worlds exists. It can be described as a sort of loosely organized spiritual government of our Milky Way galaxy.

This is a transcript of a scientific remote viewing session with a galactic federation leader [15]:

Remote Viewer

As soon as I went into his mind [a galactic federation leader], I re-emerged in space. That is where I am now. I am outside of the Milky Way, looking onto it. Dotted lines have been drawn over the image, dividing up the galaxy-like quadrants.

I am being told that there is a need for help. They need us. I am getting the sense that they need us in a galactic sense, but I seem to be resisting this. They are so much more powerful than humans; it just does not make sense why they would need us.

The leader is sensing my resistance and redirecting me to a planet. OK, I can see it is Earth. I am being told that there will be a movement off the planet in the future for humans. I am just translating the gestalts now into words. But the sense clearly is that Earth humans are violent and troublesome currently. They need shaping before a later merger. Definitely humans need to undergo some sort of change before extending far off the planet.

Monitor

Ask if there are any practical suggestions as to how we can help.

Remote Viewer

I am being told in no uncertain terms that I am to complete this book project. Others will play their parts. There are many involved. Many species representatives, groups.

Monitor

Ask who else we should meet using remote viewing, or another technique?

Remote Viewer

Only the Martians. Hmmm. I am being told that our near-term contact with extraterrestrials will be limited to the Martians for now, at least in the near future.

Monitor

Ask if there is new information that we need to know but do not know.

Remote Viewer

This fellow is very patient. He knows this is hard for me. He is telling me that many problems are coming. There definitely will be a planetary disaster, or perhaps I should say *disasters*. There will be political chaos, turbulence, an unraveling of the current political order. As we are currently, we are unable to cope with new realities. He is telling me very directly that consciousness must become a focal concern of humans in order for us to proceed further.

He is right now tapping into *your* (my monitor's) mind. It is like he is locating you, and perhaps measuring or doing something. He is telling me that you are very important in all of this. We must come back here – their world – at later dates. We will be the initial representatives of humans as determined by consciousness. He is telling me that consciousness determined our arrival point. There is more. We are not saviors, just initial representatives. He wants me to get this straight.

I am getting the sense that he wants us to understand that we have a responsibility to represent fairly. This is not to go to our heads. This is just our job now, and we all have jobs. He is also telling me that I am doing a fairly good job at writing this down.

He likes your sense of humor. He says that there will be lots of activity in the future, of the day-to-day sort. But for now, we are to focus on the book. The book is important, and they will use it.

As the transcript of this fascinating scientific remote viewing session reveals, we are in the early stages of Exopolitical research. Primary scientific databases for Exopolitical research and activity can be derived via the scientific method from a wide variety of sources, including at least the following 14 formal categories of data [16]:

A: Voluntary Conscious Physical Contactees with Off-Planet Cultures
B: Involuntary Semi-Conscious Physical Contactees (Abductees)
C: Voluntary Semi-Conscious Alter-Physical Contactees (Star People)
D: Voluntary Psychic Contactees (Channelers and Visionaries)
E: Neutral Psychic Contactees (Scientific Remote Viewers)
F: Whistle-Blowers from Inside the Secret Government
G: Documentary Evidence from Government and Official Sources
H: Superficial Excited Witnesses and Sightings Reports
I: Astute Debriefers, Debunkers, and Interpreters
J: Alien Artifacts
K: Independent Archeology, including Exo-Archaeology
L: Shamans and Occult Societies
M: Science Fiction
N: Revelations authorized by Universe Governance Bodies.

Life in the Universe

HUMANS HAVE LONG BEEN fascinated by the ultimate question, "Are we alone in the Universe?" Because of science and technology, today we are in a better position than at any other time in human history to seek the answer. Our space programs have sent probes to the outer edges of our solar system – and beyond – with messages to potential civilizations.

In 1973, when he was the Governor of Georgia, former US President Jimmy Carter filed an official report of a UFO sighting that he made in January 1969.[17] During his Presidential election campaign in May 1976, he stated: "I am convinced that UFOs exist because I've seen one."[18] Here are excerpts from two public interviews about UFOs held with Carter during the 1976 US Presidential campaign [19]:

Reporter

Governor, you once saw a UFO. If you were President, would you reopen inquiries into UFOs?

Carter

Well, no. What I would do is make information we have about those sightings available to the public... I have never tried to identify what I saw. You know, it was a light in the western sky that was very unique. I had never seen it before. There were about 20 of us who saw it. None of us could figure out what it was. I don't think it was anything solid. It was just like a light. It was a curious aberration, so I don't make fun of people who say they've see unidentified objects in the sky.

Reporter

The United States used to have a body that investigated UFOs, but that's been discontinued. Would you reopen it?

Carter

I don't know yet.

In Appleton, Wisconsin, on March 31st, 1976, a UFO expert asked Carter:

UFO Expert

Will you, as President, air what's 'behind-closed-doors' today in regards to UFOs?

Carter

Yes, I would make these kinds of data available to the public, as President, to help resolve the mystery about it.

UFO Expert

On a public basis?

Carter

Yes, on a public basis.

On June 16th, 1977, President Carter included an official statement aboard the Voyager I spacecraft for its trip outside our solar system. The Voyager statement read:

We cast this message into the Cosmos... Of the 200 billion stars in the Milky Way galaxy, some – perhaps many – may have inhabited planets and space-faring civilizations. If one such civilization intercepts Voyager and can understand these recorded contents, here is our message: We are trying to survive our time so we may live into yours. We hope someday, having solved the problems we face, to join a community of galactic civilizations. This record represents our hope and our determination and our goodwill in a vast and awesome universe. [20]

The 1977 Carter White House ET Communication Study

The Star Dreams Initiative may sound like a new initiative, but the reality is that it is based on a foundation of work that has been developing for several decades. A similar proposal was prepared for the Carter White House in 1977.

A proposed civilian scientific study of extraterrestrial communication – involving interactive communication between the terrestrial human culture and that of possible intelligent non-terrestrial civilizations – was presented to and developed with interested White House staff of the domestic policy staff of President Jimmy Carter during the period from May 1977 until the Fall of 1977. [21]

The over-all purpose of the proposed 1977 study was to create, design, and carry out an independent, civilian-led research compilation and evaluation of phenomena suggesting the presence of an extraterrestrial and/ or inter-dimensional intelligence in the near-Earth environment.

The designed outcome was to have been a public White House report, detailing the compiled evidence and evaluation, together with possible scientific models for the implications of the research. The report was to have contained public policy recommendations emerging from the evaluations and conclusions of the study. These, if warranted, included transformation of secrecy regulations of US military and intelligence agencies.

The scientific and public policy goal of the proposed 1977 Carter White House extraterrestrial communication study was to fill a substantial gap in civilian scientific knowledge of the UFO phenomenon, extraterrestrial biological entities (EBEs), and related phenomena. This knowledge gap was created and maintained by the excessive secrecy practices and regulations of the US Department of Defense, and by intelligence community UFO programs since the late 1940s, including, but not limited to, Project Grudge and Project Blue Book, as well as other alleged secret programs.

Historically, the US government and research agencies proposed for the 1977 Carter White House extraterrestrial communication study were:

The White House: Principal sponsorship and policy coordination of the proposed study.

NASA: Lead consultative agency regarding UFO and near space

phenomena, including terrestrial interaction with UFOs and EBEs.
National Science Foundation: Advice and consultation by the National
Science Board.

**Stanford Research Institute, International Center for the Study of Social
Policy:** Principal investigators, as well as scientific experts on UFOs, EBEs,
and related phenomena.

Psychological Preparation for Contact with Off-Planet Cultures

Contact with off-planet cultures would most transform our human
institutions over time – our religious traditions, economy, energy sources,
sciences, and educational system. Dr. John Mack of Harvard University
believed that politics would be changed most of all. [22] Through a properly
executed plan for Exopolitics public interest diplomacy, this transformation
can be positive and for the greater good of humanity. The process of
education about life in the Universe must continue to be gradual and focused
on spirituality in order to avoid unnecessary fear.

Michael Mannion, author of Project Mindshift, [23] explains that the US
public, and the world-at-large, have been gradually educated through the
media, including films, the print media, and television, about the possibility
of the existence of off-planet cultures. Yet, according to a Roper poll in
2002 promoted by the Coalition for Freedom of Information, 72% of US
residents believe the federal government is not telling us everything it knows
about UFOs. This would seem to suggest that public interest diplomacy
with off-planet cultures is in synch with public attitudes in the United States
and the world in general.

Highlights of the 2002 Roper Poll on UFOs and ET Life [24]

*The Roper Poll found that most US residents are psychologically and
spiritually prepared for proof of extraterrestrial life.*

...Most US residents appear comfortable with and even excited about
the thought of the discovery of extraterrestrial life. Three-quarters of
the public claim they are at least somewhat psychologically prepared
for the discovery of extraterrestrial life, and nearly half are very prepared.

...Such a discovery would not be difficult for most US residents to
reconcile with their religious beliefs. Should the government make an
announcement about the discovery of extraterrestrial life, only a very

small proportion expect it to change their religious beliefs at all.

...Furthermore, slightly more than half of US residents are at least somewhat interested in personally encountering extraterrestrial life forms here on earth. This is particularly true of males and of 18-to-24-year-olds.

Government Knows More Than It Tells Us

The majority of US respondents said they believe that their government knows more about ETs and UFOs than it is sharing with the public:

In the view of many adults (55 percent), the government does not share enough information with the public in general. An even greater proportion (roughly seven in 10) thinks that the government does not tell us everything it knows about extraterrestrial life and UFOs. The younger the age, the stronger the belief that the government is withholding information about these topics.

This is not a situation that most US residents would like to have continue. Provided national security is not at risk, most believe that the government should share information it has about other intelligent life and UFOs with the public. Males and adults below the age of 65 are more inclined to support the declassification of government information relating to such phenomena. Naturally, those with a belief and an interest in extraterrestrial life are also more likely proponents of revealing such information to the public.

The Alien Next Door?

The majority of US residents polled also said that they believe in the existence of intelligent extraterrestrial life elsewhere in the Universe:

Perhaps US residents expect to take a government announcement about extraterrestrial life in stride because many US residents already believe in the extraterrestrial. Two-thirds of US residents say they think there are other forms of intelligent life in the universe and nearly half say they believe that UFOs have visited the Earth in some form over the years (48 percent) or that aliens have monitored life on Earth (45 percent). In fact, more than one in three US residents (37 percent) believe that humans have already interacted with extraterrestrial life forms. These beliefs tend to be more prevalent among males and among adults under the age of 65.

When it comes to alien abductions, one in five US residents in general and more than half (57 percent) of those who say that humans have already interacted with extraterrestrial life believe that abductions have taken place. Once again, males and 18-to-64-year-olds are most likely to hold such a belief.

Alien Encounters

The Roper Poll found that belief in alien contact was more widespread than one might expect it to be:

One in seven US residents say that they or someone they know has had at least one "close encounter" of the "First," "Second," or "Third" kind. The largest proportion (12 percent) says they or someone else they know has seen a UFO at close range. Much smaller proportions say they or an acquaintance have seen a UFO cause a physical effect on objects, animals, or humans (three percent) or have had an encounter with extraterrestrial life (two percent). Among those who believe in abductions, one-third claim to have experienced, or know someone who experienced, a close encounter of their own.

When it comes to other unusual personal experiences, 1.4 percent, or 2.9 million US residents, say they have experienced at least four of five key events that believers of UFO abductions have identified as being of particular interest in examining whether UFO abductions might actually have taken place.

Perhaps not surprisingly, those who believe in abductions and who have experienced, or know someone who experienced, a close encounter, are more inclined to report an occurrence of at least four such events.

Integrating with an Off-Planet
Culture Now Visiting Earth

Star Dreams Mission Statement

THE EXOPOLITICAL MISSION OF a Star Dreams Initiative is to establish interactive contact through a communication protocol and engage in public interest diplomacy with one or more of the off-planet cultures that may be engaging our planet Earth at this time. Our public interest diplomacy toward off-planet cultures is a rational response to the Leaky Embargo, or the signaling by off-planet cultures of a lifting of the Universe quarantine.

"Public interest diplomacy" is a terrestrial concept developed by Western non-governmental organizations (NGOs) that established unprecedented, transparent, quasi-diplomatic relations with sectors of the Soviet state during the *glasnost* period of the 1990s. Public interest diplomacy in the form of a Star Dreams Initiative requires empathic cooperation between representatives of the mainstream terrestrial culture and a participating off-planet culture. As with *glasnost*, this cooperation can only happen through nurturing relationships between the parties. Public interest diplomacy also has as one of its goals influencing government policies so that they can be in the best interests of the human collective.

In the context of a Star Dreams Initiative, Exopolitics focuses on strategies that nurture relationships between humans and representatives of off-planet cultures, including multi-dimensional relationships founded on caring and honesty, and based on a mutual understanding of Universe reality.

The goals of public interest diplomacy include a negotiated, consensual plan for mutual, transparent, open interaction and public diplomatic relations between recognized scientific, ethical-religious, and governmental bodies of the terrestrial and specific off-planet culture(s) engaging in a Star Dreams

Initiative. This overall plan would include appropriate inter-species treaties under principles of international and universal law. Public interest diplomacy, where appropriate, may include representatives and advisory observers of galactic, interplanetary governing authorities.

A Star Dreams Initiative should develop interactive protocols, setting out the parameters of the project and appropriate proposals for outreach, contact, and public interest diplomacy. These would include interplanetary treaties establishing formal relations and detailing essential functions, such as fundamental declarations of principles governing rights, government, ownership, and other key principles of space law, bans on space weapons and warfare in space, outer space exploration standards, security, technology transfer, and interplanetary immigration.

Star Dreams protocols will be interactively published for both human and (via remote-viewing and other modalities) off-planet culture authorities. A Star Dreams Initiative would involve terrestrial and off-planet culture governing bodies:

- *Earth representatives would include:*

  United Nations Secretary-General

  United Nations Office for Outer Space Affairs

  United Nations Security Council

  United Nations General Assembly

  Member nations of the UN Committee on the Peaceful Uses of Outer Space

  Interested NGOs, educational institutions, and educational media

- *Off-planet culture representatives (via direct participation, scientific remote viewing, or other modality) would include:*

  Martian (and/or other off-planet culture) governmental authorities, as identified in scientific remote viewing sessions or other outreach modalities

  Galactic federation authorities (an interplanetary body), as identified in scientific remote viewing sessions or other outreach modalities

  Other interested off-planet culture participants, such as the Grays

Central Goals

- Transformation of the permanent warfare economy on Earth into a sustainable, cooperative, peaceful, Space Age, Universe-oriented society

- Establishing interactive, substantive communication and contact with off-planet cultures engaging our planet at this time through programmed stages of interaction

- Integration of Earth and human society into a larger, organized, advanced, spiritually developed Universe society

Design: A Functional Off-Planet Culture Landing Pad

The "Landing Pad" is a familiar archetype of today's human communities desiring to make contact with off-planet cultures. A landing pad invites the representatives of an off-planet culture to land their vehicles and interface with the human community. One such site receiving high-level, official government acknowledgment is the UFO Landing Pad in St. Paul, Alberta, Canada, which was inaugurated on June 3rd, 1967 by then-Canadian Minister of National Defense Paul Hellyer.[25]

A Star Dreams Initiative seeks to create the functional equivalent of a landing pad, for willing, interactive off-planet cultures, through the mechanism of public interest diplomacy. In the initial stages of integration with an off-planet culture, there must be a mutuality of understanding founded on interactive communication, substantive negotiations, legal norms and agreements, and plans for open, transparent, integrative relations.

Failure to move forward with an open plan to communicate with off-planet cultures and to align our government policies with universal law could result in catastrophic consequences for our world. Dire consequences for the human species may come in the form of looming ecological catastrophe on Earth, or self-destruction through nuclear annihilation, environmental warfare, or other global conflict, and the resultant breakdown in social order. One recent scientific assessment concludes that, barring substantial reduction in greenhouse gas emissions, global warming will result in the functional extinction of human civilization by the end of the 21st century.[26]

Operating from a Universal Paradigm – Empathic (Agape-Centered) Public Interest Diplomacy

Open, transparent, diplomatic dialogue between our world and off-planet cultures, by respecting universal and spiritual laws, is a necessity if our human society is to successfully come through the challenges facing it in the next decades. The protocols of communication with advanced and evolved intelligent off-planet cultures must be studied and understood.

Science is now confirming that in Universe society, love rather than conflict is the central organizing principle of advanced civilizations. One scientific remote viewer summarizes his findings, based upon interactive observations and communications via remote viewing with specific off-planet cultures, as follows:

Somehow love is the theme of God, the glue that keeps the Universe together. But only highly evolved beings realize the full extent of this reality. I do not claim to know why love is a glue of the universe. We tend to think of love as a mushy emotion. My remote viewing of highly evolved beings suggests that the human concept of love is very primitive, but I really do not know of any other word to describe the flavor of what I sense. Whatever love is in these evolved beings, it is not mushy. It is matched with clear thinking and effective action. There is a smoothness in their lives that is enviable.[27]

The lack of empathetic public interest diplomacy by human representatives may be one key reason why there has been no public, sustained official contact by off-planet cultures with official representatives of Earth, except for spiritual remote viewers. To achieve authentic, empathic communication of the sort required for public interest diplomacy, Earth representatives must open themselves up to the experiences of spirituality and agape (cosmic love). Remote viewing modalities offer science-based protocols for multi-dimensional interactive contact with higher evolved intelligences.

Human fear can block the multi-dimensional communication process with higher, evolved multi-dimensional intelligences. Pierre Juneau, the Canadian Exopolitics advisor, states that exopolitical diplomacy requires...

...a vibrational synchronicity with those we are communicating with and must be nurtured within the diplomats representing the peoples of

Earth… Personal growth and personal transformation is essential. Where we are at spiritually (love) seems to determine our capability to interact directly or via telepathy with higher intelligences. Dr. John Mack's research… demonstrated that different experiencers had different experiences with the "multi-dimensional ET beings" that often seem to mirror the experiencer's vibrational energy or spiritual level. I therefore feel that a Star Dreams Initiative must encourage both Exopolitics diplomats and society as a whole to focus on love, caring, compassion, and trust in universal law, trust in God/source, as the foundation of our interactions with off-planet cultures.[28]

Banning Weapons and Warfare in Space

One thing is clear: Humanity will not be allowed to venture out into the Universe as a war-like species. Together, we can put an end to the highly profitable war industry by putting our differences aside and working together to present win-win solutions to decision makers. Before we rejoin Universe society, humanity must ban space weapons and warfare in space and not expand our permanent war economy into space.

A coordinated strategy to get world leaders to sign a treaty banning space weapons will put a lid on the war economy. It will result in a sustainable, cooperative, democratic Space Age society that goes beyond fear and focuses on honoring all life on our planet and in our universe, instead of destroying it. With today's technology, a peace-based economy can be just as viable, if not more viable, than a war-based one.

Humans can resolve international conflicts through advanced, non-violent conflict resolution techniques: empathy instead of force; better communications and the art of diplomacy; understanding the deeper causes of conflicts. We can, in lateral application, transform the war industry into a sustainable, peaceful space exploration society.

New Energy

Public interest diplomacy with off-planet cultures complements the goals of the Disclosure Movement, which seeks the release of reverse-engineered extraterrestrial energy, propulsion, and other technologies allegedly held in secret by certain terrestrial governments, most notably the US government.[29] Unless humanity commits more resources to exploring and integrating new, sustainable, clean energy sources, we will face catastrophic environmental disasters in the coming future. Many of our potentially unsolvable ecological challenges can be partially resolved through the solutions that will result from a Star Dreams Initiative. Through the acquisition, reverse engineering, manufacture, and integration of advanced technologies from off-planet cultures, we can replace fossil fuels and stem the global climate change that the greenhouse gases that they produce cause.

Exopolitics and Human Perception

Terrestrial politics will be changed most of all by our contact with an off-planet culture. Exopolitics, as a discipline, is the study of politics, government, and law in the Universe. It includes the study of political, governmental, and legal aspects of interactive contact and social integration between humans and off-planet cultures on Earth, in space, or through multi-dimensional realities. The exopolitical model provides an operational bridge between models of terrestrial politics, government, and law, and the larger models of politics, government, and law in Universe society.

One of the challenges in basic Exopolitics research is that information derived from apparent contact with off-planet cultures has been so compartmentalized that each person involved looks at the phenomenon from his or her unique, and at times, limited perspective. For example, scientific remote viewers have a different model of perception than that of military and intelligence agencies. The military appears to operate from a variety of different models of perception, ranging from perceiving inter-active communication with off-planet cultures as a national security threat to perceiving the phenomenon as an opportunity for institutional evolution. Likewise, scientists have their own models, as do Ufologists, alien abduction researchers, conspiracists, experiencers (including alien abductees), native peoples, and religious or spiritually oriented observers. Perceptions vary according to what part of the world the observer comes from, as well as that culture's history and myths.

Exopolitics and Earth's Looming Ecological Emergency

Earth's best exopolitical strategy for surviving its looming ecological emergency is to integrate with spiritually advanced off-planet cultures now visiting Earth. We must seek multilateral, interplanetary, and Universe government assistance in transforming our present permanent warfare economy and fossil fuel-nuclear civilization into a sustainable, cooperative, Universe-oriented society. The Leaky Embargo strategy and scientific remote viewing data have given us a working critical path. We can begin outreach to the apparent off-planet culture on Mars. In parallel, we can outreach to other ethical, spiritually advanced off-planet cultures now visiting Earth.

Intentional contact and interrelation with a Mars-based (or other) off-planet culture could impact positively our transformation of the permanent war economy on Earth into a peaceful, sustainable, cooperative Space Age one. Contact with a possible Martian civilization could aid in our terrestrial society's integration into Universe society. Because of the ecological cataclysms Mars has suffered in the past, Martian society is focused on environmental survival. Mars is astronomically relatively close to our planet. If the preliminary scientific remote viewing data are correct, and Martian civilization *is* about 150 years in advance of Earth's current development, Martian society may have developed key technologies for space travel and clean energy production. A Martian civilization's proximity to Earth is highly fortuitous. Having survived a planetary cataclysm on its home planet, Mars, Martian society may be able to teach our terrestrial civilization how to cope with looming ecological emergencies on Earth.

Human exopolitical acknowledgment that off-planet cultures are visiting Earth comes at the same time as a well-founded scientific prediction that humanity – or the present human civilization – may be extinct by the end of the 21st century. Professor Peter Barrett, Ph.D., director of Victoria University's Antarctic Research Center, warns that climate change is a major threat to our planet:

> After 40 years, I'm part of a huge community of scientists who have become alarmed with our discovery that we know from our knowledge of the ancient past, that if we continue our present growth path, we are facing extinction... Not in millions of years, or even millennia, but by the end of the 21st century.[30]

The scientific basis for this potentially cataclysmic warming of the Earth's climate is confirmed by reports of the Intergovernmental Panel on Climate Change, an international body of over 1,000 climate scientists from 100 countries that is considered the world's most authoritative source of information on global warming. Emission of greenhouse gases caused by human consumption of fossil fuels, it believes, may lead to a peak in the Earth's temperature to the same level of global warming that it had 35 million years ago, before the appearance of ice sheets in Antarctica.[31]

A recent climate change study commissioned by the US Department of Defense concludes that abrupt climate change and ensuing environmental and social emergencies may accelerate on Earth as soon as the period 2015 to 2020. The collapse of the ocean conveyer climate system is predicted to accelerate abrupt climate change, resulting in food and water shortage, and massive population dislocations.[32]

Unless a global strategy for reduction in carbon dioxide emissions is undertaken, humanity may well destroy its own civilization by the end of the 21st century. It appears that the United States, which has been leading the opposition to global controls on carbon dioxide emissions and accounts for about four percent (4%) of the global population, by some reports produces up to one-third (30-35%) of the world's greenhouse gases.[33] Moreover, ecological catastrophe caused by nuclear winter resulting from an intentional or accidental nuclear war, or environmental warfare, such as seismic or climate warfare, would also produce further ecological crisis on Earth.

A lifting of the planetary quarantine could not come at a more fortuitous time for humanity. The synchronicities between the lifting of Earth's quarantine, through a Leaky Embargo strategy, and the threat of human extinction, resulting from environmental catastrophe on Earth, are remarkable. In the very time period that our fossil-fuel nuclear civilization could cause our extinction, humanity has available to it the tools for public interest diplomacy with off-planet cultures, which could well be instrumental in helping Earth's transformation and survival into a universal future.

Some scientific remote viewing data developed in the 1990s indicate that humankind may not be able to forestall the major effects of this coming ecological catastrophe, and may suffer a large population die-off. These specific data indicate that the galactic federation will not intervene to facilitate humanity's survival of the coming ecological catastrophes. The galactic federation sees these self-induced ecological catastrophes as necessary for humanity's long-term evolution. They will cause us to acknowledge our shortsighted exploitation of the Earth's resources and our many social dysfunctions, and then permit us to build anew after a considerable period of soul-searching.[34]

Under this scenario, surviving humans may be forced beneath the surface of the Earth, in underground structures, for several centuries, until the Earth's climate comes back into balance. If this is our fate, humanity may be helped in this scenario by integration with an off-planet culture on Mars that can teach us how to survive underground on Earth, which is how the Martian civilization has survived since the cataclysmic destruction of its environment.

It is a scientific principle that we can change our collective future. We humans do not have to acquiesce in a die-off scenario, brought about solely because the greedy human plutocracy and permanent war economy encourage humanity to continue to consume fossil fuels and accelerate climate shift through greenhouse gas emissions.

Exopolitics is providing us with another avenue, one of transformation to a sustainable, Universe-oriented society. Once you and I are made aware of alternative futures, we can choose and mobilize towards a positive future here on Earth.

Choose to transform Earth into a Universe-oriented society, without the unnecessary trauma of a human near-extinction. Exopolitics is our bridge to Universe society, our future home. Invite all of humanity and our visiting, spiritually advanced off-planet cultures to participate in the Star Dreams Initiative.

We are entering a new domain of politics. We are shifting from a terrestrial-bound community to a Universe-directed body politic, which is our fundamental cosmic right. The transformation starts within each of us, for we ourselves are the universal transformation. We, the people, are the new universal human beings. We are only at the beginning of our exploration of the Universe.

Join in the vision of a Decade of Contact in all nations, a transformation of our human self-image. The Decade of Contact will be a proactive, education-based process of global integration with Universe society. Our entire terrestrial fabric – governmental, scientific, technological, philosophical, educational, energetic, and environmental – calls out for a new Universe-based reality. Let us save our precious Earth. Together, let us create a new vision, a planetary campaign for a Universe-based civilization.

Appendix

A Chronology of Statements about Extraterrestrial Contact

The statements of many prominent government officials, military officers, astronauts, scientists, educators, researchers, and others offer ample evidence that off-planet cultures are visiting our planet and engaging our civilization.

General Nathan D. Twining, Chief of Staff of the US Air Force and Chairman of the Joint Chiefs of Staff [1957-1960], in a letter to Brigadier General George Schulgen, Chief of Air Force Intelligence and Commanding General of the Army Air Forces, dated September 23rd, 1947:

The phenomenon reported is something real and not visionary or fictitious. There are objects, probably approximating the shape of a disc, of such appreciable size as to appear to be as large as a man-made aircraft. The reported operating characteristics, such as extreme rates of climb, maneuverability (particularly in roll), and action which must be considered evasive when sighted or contacted by friendly aircraft and radar, lend belief to the possibility that some of the objects are controlled, either manually, automatically, or remotely. The common description of the objects is metallic or light reflecting surface, circular or elliptical in shape, flat on bottom and domed on top.

Brigadier General George Schulgen, in a Draft Intelligence Collections Memorandum about the Roswell Incident, dated October 28th, 1947:

It is the considered opinion of some elements that the object [recovered at Roswell] may in fact represent an interplanetary craft of some kind.

General Robert B. Landry, US Air Force attaché to President Truman, about an experience he had while serving in the Truman administration in 1948:

I was called one afternoon to come to the Oval Office – the President wanted to see me... I was directed to report quarterly to the President after consulting with Central Intelligence people, as to whether or not any UFO incidents received by them could be considered as having any strategic threatening implications.

Air Technical Intelligence Center, *Estimate of the Situation*, the final report by Project Sign to the Pentagon about the origin of the UFO mystery, 1948:

Flying saucers are probably real extraterrestrial spacecraft.

The Federal Bureau of Investigation, in a memorandum about unidentified flying objects promulgated by the FBI in 1949:

Army intelligence has recently said that the matter of 'Unidentified Aircraft' or 'Unidentified Aerial Phenomena,' otherwise known as 'Flying Discs,' 'Flying Saucers,' and 'Balls of Fire,' is considered Top Secret by intelligence officers of both the Army and the Air Forces.

Harry S. Truman, 33rd President of the United States [1945-53], in a comment made at a White House press conference held in Washington on April 4th, 1950:

I can assure you that flying saucers, given that they exist, are not constructed by any power on Earth.

A US Air Force intelligence report that was prepared following the reported sighting of a UFO by the American pilot of a P-51 jet airplane in 1951:

[Object was] described as flat on top and bottom and appearing from a front view to have round edges and [be] slightly beveled... No vapor trails or exhaust or visible means of propulsion. Described as traveling at tremendous speed... Pilot considered by associates to be highly reliable, of mature judgment, and a creditable observer.

Dr. Donald "Deke" Slayton, US Air Force test pilot and Mercury astronaut, in 1951:

I was testing a P-51 fighter... when I spotted this object. I was at about 10,000 feet on a nice, bright, sunny afternoon. I thought the object was a kite, then, I realized that no kite is going to fly that high. As I got closer it looked like a weather balloon, gray and about three feet in diameter. But as soon as I got behind the darn thing it didn't look like a balloon anymore. It looked like a saucer, a disk. About the same time, I realized that it was suddenly going way from me and there I was, running at about 300 miles per hour. I tracked it for a little way, and then all of a sudden the damn thing just took off. It pulled about a 45-degree climbing turn and accelerated and just flat disappeared.

Dr. Walter Reidel, prominent German rocket expert, quoted in LIFE, on April 7th, 1952:

I'm convinced that [flying] saucers have an out-of-world basis.

Harry G. Barnes, air traffic controller, describing the UFOs tracked on radar at 7,000 miles per hour that hovered over Washington, DC in July 1952:

For six hours... there were at least 10 unidentifiable objects moving above Washington. They were not ordinary aircraft.

The American pilot of an F-94 jet airplane, upon being debriefed following his mid-air encounter with an unidentified flying object, flying at great speed, in 1952:

Based on my experience in fighter tactics, it is my opinion that the object was controlled by something having visual contact with us. The power and acceleration were beyond the capability of any known US aircraft.

Brigadier General João Adil Oliveira, Chief of Brazil's Air Force General Staff Information Service, in a briefing to the Army War College held in 1954:

The problem of 'flying discs' has polarized the attention of the whole world, but it's serious and it deserves to be treated seriously. Almost all the governments of the great powers are interested in it, dealing with it in a serious and confidential manner, due to its military interest.

Brigadier General Oliveira, again addressing the UFO subject, this time in 1958:

It is impossible to deny any more the existence of flying saucers at the present time. The flying saucer is not a ghost from another dimension... It is a fact confirmed by material evidence.

HRH Prince Philip, the Duke of Edinburgh, in a comment about flying saucers published in the *Sunday Dispatch*, London, on March 28th, 1954:

There are many reasons to believe that they [UFOs] do exist. There is so much evidence from reliable witnesses.

Air Chief Marshal Lord Dowding, commanding officer of the Royal Air Force during World War II, in the *Sunday Dispatch*, London, on July 11th, 1954:

More than 10,000 sightings have been reported, the majority of which cannot be accounted for by any 'scientific' explanation.

I am convinced that these objects do exist and that they are not manufactured by any nation on Earth. I can therefore see no alternative to accepting the theory that they come from some extraterrestrial source.

Lord Dowding, later quoted by the Reuters news agency, in August 1954:

Of course the flying saucers are real, and they are interplanetary.

Professor Hermann Oberth, a founder of modern astronautics, in an article about UFOs published in *American Weekly* magazine, on October 24th, 1954:

It is my thesis that flying saucers are real and that they are space ships from another solar system. I think that they possibly are manned by intelligent observers who are members of a race that may have been investigating our Earth for centuries.

...UFOs are conceived and directed by intelligent beings of a very high order, and they are propelled by distorting the gravitational field, converting gravity into usable energy... There is no doubt in my mind that these objects are interplanetary craft of some sort...

...My colleagues and I are confident that they do not originate in our solar system, but we feel that they may use Mars or some other body as sort of a way station. They probably do not originate in our solar system, perhaps not even in our galaxy.

Dr. Carl Gustav Jung, founder of Jungian psychology and a pioneer of psychiatry, in an article published in *Flying Saucer Review* in 1955:

A purely psychological explanation is ruled out... The discs show signs of intelligent guidance, by quasi-human pilots.

Senator Richard Russell, chair of the US Senate Armed Services Committee, regarding his sighting of a UFO during a visit to the former Soviet Union in 1955:

I have discussed this matter with the affected agencies of the government, and they are of the opinion that it is not wise to publicize this matter at this time.

Allen W. Dulles, Director of Central Intelligence, Central Intelligence Agency [1953-61], in a statement regarding CIA policy about UFOs that he made in 1955:

Maximum security exists concerning the subject of UFOs.

Admiral Delmar Fahrney, head, guided-missile program, US Navy, in a letter to the National Investigations Committee on Aerial Phenomena (NICAP), sent in 1956:

Unidentified flying objects are entering our atmosphere at very high speeds and obviously under intelligent control. We must solve this riddle without delay...

Admiral Fahrney, quoted a year later in the *New York Times*, in 1957:

No agency in this country or Russia is able to duplicate at this time the speeds and accelerations which radars and observers indicate these flying objects are able to achieve... Reliable reports indicate there are objects coming into our atmosphere at very high speeds and controlled by thinking intelligences.

General Lionel M. Chassin, Commanding General of France's Air Force and General Air Defense Coordinator of the Allied Air Forces of NATO, in 1958:

The number of thoughtful, intelligent, educated people in full possession of their faculties who have seen something and described it grows every day... We can say categorically that mysterious objects have indeed appeared and continue to appear in the sky that surrounds us.

US Representative William H. Ayres, describing US Congressional attention to the subject of unidentified flying objects, in a statement made in 1958:

Congressional investigations... are still being held on the problem of unidentified flying objects and the problem is one in which there is quite a bit of interest.

...Since most of the material presented to the committees is classified, [transcripts of] the hearings are never printed. ·

Dr. Wernher von Braun, famed rocketry pioneer and aeronautical engineer, Director of NASA [1960-70], commenting about the UFO enigma in 1959:

We find ourselves faced by powers which are far stronger than we had hitherto assumed, and whose base is at present unknown to us. More I cannot say at present.

...We are now engaged in entering into closer contact with those powers, and in six or nine months time it may be possible to speak with some precision on the matter...

Lt. Colonel Richard Headrick, USAF, bombing radar expert, in a statement about UFOs that he observed while serving in the United States military in 1959:

Saucers exist – I saw two. They were intelligently flown or operated – [for they showed] evasive tactics, formation flight, hovering. They were mechanisms, not United States weapons, nor Russian. I presume they are extraterrestrial.

Vice Admiral Roscoe H. Hillenkoetter, first Director of the CIA [1947-1950], in a signed statement to the US Congress, dated August 22nd, 1960:

Behind the scenes, high-ranking Air Force officers are soberly concerned about the UFOs. But through official secrecy and ridicule, many citizens are led to believe the unknown flying objects are nonsense. To hide the facts, the Air Force has silenced its personnel... I urge immediate Congressional action to reduce the dangers from secrecy about unidentified flying objects.

Astronaut M. Scott Carpenter, who photographed an unidentified flying object while in Earth orbit during the Mercury 7 mission on May 24th, 1962:

At no time when the astronauts were in space were they alone; there was a constant surveillance by UFOs.

Major Robert White, USAF test pilot, about a UFO he saw at 58 miles above Earth, during an X-15 test flight that he made on July 17th, 1962:

I have no idea what it could be... [It was] grayish in colour and about 30 to 40 feet away.

Albert M. Chop, Deputy Public Relations Director for NASA, quoted in an article in *True* magazine published in January 1965:

I've been convinced for a long time that the flying saucers are interplanetary. We are being watched by beings from outer space.

Journalist John G. Fuller, author of *Incident at Exeter* and *The Interrupted Journey*, two landmark investigations of alien-human contact, writing in 1965:

[F]ighters are constantly scrambled to pursue these objects...

Professor Claudio Anguila, director of the Cerro Calan Observatory, as quoted by the Reuters news agency on August 26th, 1965:

We are not alone in the Universe.

Gerald R. Ford, 38th President of the United States [1974-77], in a letter sent to L. Mendel Rivers, Chairman of the US House Armed Services Committee, dated March 28th, 1966:

In the firm belief that the American public deserves a better explanation than has thus far been given by the Air Force, I strongly recommend that there be a committee investigation of the UFO phenomenon. I think we owe it to the people to establish credibility regarding UFOs and to produce the greatest possible enlightenment on this subject.

Excerpt from a classified report by a US Air Force Strike Team located at Minot Air Force Base, near Minot, North Dakota, in 1966:

When the team was about 10 miles from the landing site, static disrupted radio contact with them. Five to eight minutes later, the glow diminished, and the UFO took off. Another UFO was visually sighted and confirmed by radar.

General Kanshi Ishikawa, Chief of Staff, Japan's Air Self-Defense Force (ASDF), Chitose Air Base, in a statement about UFOs made in 1967:

UFOs have been tracked by radar; so, UFOs are real and they may come from outer space... UFO photographs and various materials show scientifically that there are more advanced people piloting the saucers and mother ships...

Dr. James E. McDonald, prominent astrophysicist, in a letter that he wrote to U Thant, who was then Secretary-General of the United Nations, in 1967:

It is my present opinion... that the most probable assumption to account for the phenomenon of the UFOs is that these are... of extraterrestrial origin.

Dr. James E. McDonald, in testimony before a US House subcommittee investigating the phenomenon of unidentified flying objects, in 1968:

My own present opinion... is that UFOs are probably extraterrestrial devices engaged in something that might very tentatively be termed surveillance.

Colonel Fujio Hayashi, commander of the Air Transport Wing of the Japanese Air Self-Defense Force (ASDF), in a statement made sometime during the 1960s:

UFOs are impossible to deny... It is very strange that we have never been able to find out the source for over two decades.

Astronaut Edgar D. Mitchell, Apollo 14, sixth human to walk on the Moon, founder, the Institute of Noetic Sciences (IONS), in a statement made in 1971:

We all know UFOs are real. All we need to ask is, where are they from?

Astronaut Eugene Cernan, the commander of Apollo 17, in a personal observation published on the pages of the *Los Angeles Times* in 1973:

I've been asked about UFOs and I've said publicly I thought they were somebody else, some other civilization.

Ronald W. Reagan, 40th President of the United States [1981-89], describing a sighting of a UFO that he had while Governor of California in 1974:

I was in a plane last week when I looked out the window and saw this white light. It was zigzagging around. I went up to the pilot and said, 'Have you ever seen anything like that?' He was shocked and he said, 'Nope.' And I said to him, 'Let's follow it!' We followed it for several minutes. It was a bright white light. We followed it to Bakersfield, and all of a sudden to our utter amazement it went straight up into the heavens. When I got off the plane I told Nancy all about it. But we didn't file a report on the object because for a long time they considered you a nut if you saw a UFO.

Dr. Margaret Mead, world-renowned anthropologist and author, in an article published in the popular American magazine for women, *Redbook*, in 1974:

There are UFOs. That is, there is a hard core of cases – perhaps 20 to 30 percent in different studies – for which there is no explanation... We can only imagine what purpose lies behind the activities of these quiet, harmlessly cruising objects that time and again approach the Earth. The most likely explanation, it seems to me, is that they are simply watching what we are up to.

M. Robert Galley, French Minister of Defense, in a radio interview during which UFO intelligence data gathered by France was discussed, in 1974:

[I]f listeners could see for themselves the mass of reports coming in from the airborne gendarmerie [a form of militarily armed police], from the mobile gendarmerie, and from the gendarmerie charged with the job of conducting investigations, all of which reports are forwarded by us to the National Center for Space Studies, then they would see that it is all pretty disturbing.

Dr. Claude Poher, founder, GEPAN, the UFO investigation office of France's National Center for Space Sciences, about sightings in France, 1974-78:

Taking into account the facts that we have gathered from the observers and from the location of their observations, we concluded that there generally can be said to be a material phenomenon behind the observations. In 60% of the cases... the description of this phenomenon is apparently one of a flying machine whose origin, modes of lifting, and/or propulsion are totally outside our knowledge.

Senator Barry Goldwater, Republican candidate for President of the United States in 1964, in a letter to researcher Shlomo Arnon of UCLA, dated March 28th, 1975:

The subject of UFOs is one that has interested me for some time. About 10 or 12 years ago, I made an effort to find out what was in the building at Wright Patterson Air Force Base, where the information is stored that has been collected by the Air Force, and I was understandably denied the request. It is still classified above Top Secret.

Jimmy Carter, 39th President of the United States [1977-81], quoted in the American press on June 8th, 1976, and later confirmed by Jim Purks:

If I become President, I'll make every piece of information this country has about UFO sightings available to the public, and the scientists. I am convinced that UFOs exist because I've seen one.

General Carlos Castro Cavero, former Commander of Spain's Third Aerial Region, in an interview with Spanish writer J. J. Benitez on June 27th, 1976:

I believe that UFOs are spaceships or extraterrestrial craft... The nations of the world are currently working together in the investigation of the UFO phenomenon. There is an international exchange of data. Maybe when this group of nations acquires more precise and definite information, it will be possible to release the news to the world.

Lieutenant General Akira Hirano, Chief of Staff, Japan's Air Self-Defense Force, in a public statement about UFO's made in September 1977:

We frequently see unidentified objects in the sky. We are quietly investigating them.

Major L. Gordon Cooper, USAF, Mercury and Gemini astronaut, in a letter to Grenada's Ambassador to the United Nations, dated

November 9th, 1978:

I believe that these extraterrestrial vehicles and their crews are visiting this planet from other planets, which obviously are a little more technically advanced than we are here on Earth. I feel that we need to have a top-level, coordinated program to scientifically collect and analyze data from all over the Earth concerning any type of encounter, and to determine how best to interface with these visitors in a friendly fashion.

Russian Cosmonaut Victor Afanasyev, describing an unidentified flying object that he saw while aboard the Solyut 6 space station in April 1979:

It followed us during half of our orbit. We observed it on the light side, and when we entered the shadow side, it disappeared completely. It was an engineered structure, made from some type of metal, [about] 40 meters long with inner hulls. The object was narrow here and wider here, and inside there were openings. Some places had projections like small wings. The object stayed very close to us. We photographed it, and our photos showed it to be 23 to 28 meters away.

Victor Marchetti, former Special Assistant to the Executive Director of the CIA, in an article, "How the CIA Views the UFO Phenomenon," published in May 1979:

We have, indeed, been contacted – perhaps even visited – by extraterrestrial beings, and the US government, in collusion with the other national powers of the Earth, is determined to keep this information from the general public.

Azim Daudpota, Air Marshal of Zimbabwe, commenting about a UFO seen by numerous witnesses while simultaneously tracked on radar in 1985:

This was no ordinary UFO. Scores of people saw it. It was no illusion, no deception, no imagination.

Lord Hill-Norton, Chief of Defense Staff, UK Ministry of Defense [1971-73], Chairman, Military Committee of NATO [1974-77], in his Foreword to Timothy Good's leading history about UFO cases, *Above Top Secret*, published in 1988:

The evidence that there are objects which have been seen in our atmosphere, and even on terra firma, that cannot be accounted for either as man-made objects or as any physical force or effect known to our scientists seems to me to be overwhelming.

...A very large number of sightings have been vouched for by persons whose credentials seem to me unimpeachable. It is striking that so many have been trained observers, such as police officers and airline or military pilots. Their observations have in many instances – though by no means a majority – been supported by technical means such as radar or, even more convincingly, by visible evidence of the condition of the observers or – and this is common to many events – interference with electrical apparatus of one sort or another... It is difficult to credit that they have all been either lying or hallucinating.

...From the earliest days of the modern outbreak of sightings some 40 years ago, there is a quite remarkable similarity between the descriptions given by observers of the flying vehicles. It is the more remarkable that there have been tens of thousands of these reports, from observers who range from illiterate peasants in Argentina and Spain to people with Ph.D.s in other countries and they have all been given spontaneously – which has led to the generic term "flying saucer." It must be more than a coincidence.

Toshiki Kaifu, Prime Minister of Japan, in a letter to the Mayor of Hakui City, Japan, dated June 24th, 1990:

I believe it is a reasonable time to take the UFO problem seriously as a reality.

Major-General Wilfred de Brouwer, Deputy Chief of the Royal Belgian Air Force, as reported by the UFO research organization, SOBEPS, in 1991:

A certain number of anomalous phenomena have been produced within

Belgian airspace... A certain number of unauthorized aerial activities have taken place.

...The day will come undoubtedly when the phenomenon will be observed with technological means of detection and collection that won't leave a single doubt about its origin. This should lift a part of the veil that has covered the mystery for a long time – a mystery that continues to the present. But it exists, it is real, and that in itself is an important conclusion.

John E. Mack, M.D., professor of psychiatry at Harvard College, Pulitzer Prize winner, champion of the proposition that the alien abduction phenomenon is based in reality, author of *Abduction: Human Encounters with Aliens*, in 1994:

I will stress once again that we do not know the source from which the UFOs or the alien beings come (whether or not, for example, they originate in the physical Universe as modern astrophysics has described it). But they manifest in the physical world and bring about definable consequences in that domain.

Dr. Brian O'Leary, former astronaut, astronomy professor at Cornell University, and physics professor at Princeton University, on September 18th, 1994:

For nearly 50 years, the secrecy apparatus within the United States government has kept from the public UFO and alien contact information... We *have* contact with alien cultures.

Walter H. Andrus, Jr., International Director, Mutual UFO Network (MUFON), quoted in Ronald Story, *The Encyclopedia of Extraterrestrial Encounters*, in 2000:

After... interviewing several hundred witnesses to UFO sightings, reviewing the 1,600 UFO landing trace cases compiled by Ted Phillips, and reading the 1,800 humanoid or entity cases collected by Ted Bloecher, my initial conclusion is that our Earth is being visited by entities from an advanced intelligence in their spacecraft conducting a surveillance of life on this planet.

Jerome Clark, UFO researcher and editor, Center for UFO Studies (CUFOS), quoted in Ronald Story, *The Encyclopedia of Extraterrestrial Encounters,* **in 2000:**

After a lifetime in this subject, I have concluded that the extraterrestrial hypothesis is one reasonable tentative approach to putting the best-documented and most puzzling UFO reports into a scientifically defensible conceptual framework. By such reports I mean those with credible multiple or independent witnesses, instrumented observations, and physical evidence.

Raymond Fowler, UFO researcher and author of eight books in Ufology, quoted in Ronald Story, *The Encyclopedia of Extraterrestrial Encounters,* **in 2000:**

After years of study and personal on-site investigation of UFO reports, I am certain that there is more than ample high-quality observational evidence from highly trained and reliable lay witnesses to indicate that there are unidentified machine-like objects under intelligent control operating in our atmosphere. Such evidence in some cases is supported by anomalous physical effects upon the witnesses, electrical devices, and the environment, as well as by instrumentation such as radar and Geiger counters.

Leslie Kean, in "Science and the Failure to Investigate Unidentified Aerial Phenomena," a research report commissioned by the SCI-FI channel, 2002:

Unidentified aerial phenomena, otherwise known as UFOs, are real, not the stuff of science fiction. Something for which there is no scientific explanation has been observed in America's (and the world's) air space for over 55 years. Trained observers – pilots, air traffic controllers, radar operators, astronauts, military personnel – and government agencies have reported and documented spectacular events visually, photographically, and on radar.

Francis L. Ridge, National Investigations Committee on Aerial Phenomena (NICAP), on the extensive amount of UFO evidence that today exists, in 2004:

There have been millions of UFO sightings... We have on record 100,000-plus sightings... [W]e have 3,000-plus sightings from aircraft... Over 200 cases involving a nuclear connection... 500 radar cases... Photographic evidence, 4,770 cases... Humanoid cases, hundreds... 5,600 physical trace cases documented, 4,104 involving UFO visual sightings... Over a hundred cases of UFO sightings involving animal reactions... Over 500 cases [of electro-magnetic effects] associated with UFO sightings... Hundreds, if not thousands, of excellent close encounters by credible observers whose testimony in court would be taken at face value... About 1,500 UNKNOWNS listed in Project Blue Book files.

Michael Hesemann, author and one of Europe's leading UFO researchers, quoted by UFO researcher Rajesh Kumar, at www.ufoevidence.org, in 2005:

After investigating the UFO phenomenon all over the world, after studying thousands of pages of released government documents, and interviewing eyewitnesses and insiders, including generals, intelligence officers, cosmonauts, and astronauts, military and commercial pilots, I do not have the shadow of a doubt anymore that we are indeed visited by extraterrestrial intelligences.

...We have to learn to deal with this situation and prepare for contact. Studying the behaviour pattern of the phenomenon, I have come to the conclusion that they are neither friend nor foe, but study our planet and civilization from a mainly scientific perspective. They are as curious to learn more about us, as we would love to study other human and humanoid civilizations.

...A contact with an extraterrestrial civilization is the greatest challenge for mankind in the Third Millennium. We would finally realize that we are indeed not alone, which could cause a new Copernican revolution, a quantum leap in our thinking and perspective. We would finally realize that we are one mankind and all the small differences that separate humans from each other today – nationality, race, and religion – would disappear. Only together can mankind explore the Universe, our true home and destiny.

Selected
Exopolitical References

Exopolitics, Climate Change, and Ecological Catastrophe

SCHWARTZ, Peter, and RANDALL, Doug, "An Abrupt Climate Change Scenario and Its Implications for United States National Security," Emeryville, CA, Global Business Network, October 2003.

BARRETT, Peter, "The basis for the claim that 'we are facing the end of civilisation as we know it... by the end of the century'," Wellington, NZ, Antarctic Research Center, Victoria University, 2004.

WORLD METEOROLOGICAL ORGANIZATION, INTERGOVERN-MENTAL PANEL ON CLIMATE CHANGE (IPCC), *IPCC Third Assessment Report – Climate Change 2001*, Cambridge, UK, Cambridge University Press, 2001.

The Kyoto Protocol to the United Nations Framework Convention on Climate Change, Kyoto, Japan, December 11, 1997, at www.unfccc.int/resource/docs/convkp/kpeng.pdf.

KAPLAN, Stephen, "The Launching of the New Energy Movement," New Energy Movement, 2004, at *exopolitics*.blogs.com/exopolitics/2004/05/the_launching_o.html.

Exopolitics and Off-Planet Cultures

DEARDORFF, James, HAISCH, Bernard, MACCABEE, Bruce, and
PUTHOFF, Hal E., "Inflation-Theory Implications for
Extraterrestrial Visitation," *Journal of the British Interplanetary
Society*, vol. 58, 2005, pp. 43-50.

KAKU, Michio, "The Physics of Extra-Terrestrial Civilizations. *How
advanced could they possibly be?"* at www.mkaku.org/articles/
physics_of_alien_civs.shtml, 2005.

NATIONAL AERONAUTICS AND SPACE ADMINISTRATION
(NASA), "Scientists Discover First of a New Class of Extrasolar
Planets," Houston, TX, August 31st, 2004.

TAYLOR, Greg, "Co-Founder of String Field Theory Explores the Physics
of ET," www.space.com, October 30th, 2003.

DAVID, Leonard, "UFO Group Demands Congressional Hearing,"
www.space.com, May 9th, 2001.

CAMERON, Grant, "UFO Studies Done and Proposed by the Carter
Administration," www.presidentialufo.com, 2005.

THE ROPER POLL, *UFOs and Extraterrestrial Life: Americans' Beliefs
and Personal Experiences,* prepared for the SCI-FI Channel,
September 2002.

SALLA, Michael E., *Exopolitics: Political Implications of the
Extraterrestrial Presence*, Tempe, AZ, Dandelion Books, 2003.

MACK, John E., *Passport to the Cosmos: Human Transformation and
Alien Encounters*, New York, NY, Crown Publishers, 1999.

JUNG, Carl G., "Dr. Carl Jung on Unidentified Flying Objects," *Flying Saucer Review*, vol. 1, no. 2, 1955.

DISCLOSURE PROJECT, "Disclosure, Military and Government Witnesses Reveal the Greatest Secrets in Modern History," The Disclosure Project, Crozet, VA, 2001.

BATEMAN, Wesley H., *Through Alien Eyes*, Sedona, AZ, Light Technology Publishing, 2000.

ANONYMOUS, *The Urantia Book*, Chicago, IL, The Urantia Foundation, 1955.

MANNION, Michael, *Project Mindshift: The Re-education of the American Public Concerning Extraterrestrial Life*, New York, NY, M. Evans and Company, 1998.

BOURDAIS, Gildas, COMETA: The French Report on UFOs and Defense: a Summary, Chicago, IL, Center for UFO Studies (CUFOS), 1999.

Exopolitics and Scientific Remote Viewing

BROWN, Courtney, *Cosmic Explorers*, New York, NY, Dutton, 1999.

___. *Cosmic Voyage*, New York, NY, Dutton, 1996.

PUTHOFF, Hal E., "CIA-initiated Remote Viewing at Stanford Research Institute," Austin, TX, Institute for Advanced Studies, 1995.

LORA, Doris, and TARG, Russell, "How I was a Psychic Spy for the CIA and found God," Institute for Noetic Sciences (IONS), November 2003.

TARG, Russell, and KATRA, Jane, "The Scientific and Spiritual Implications of Psychic Abilities," Palo Alto, CA, at www.espresearch.com/espgeneral/doc-AT.shtml, 2005.

Exopolitics and the United Nations

RECOMMENDATION TO ESTABLISH UN AGENCY FOR UFO RESEARCH – UN General Assembly decision 33/426, 1978.

COOPER, L. Gordon, "Astronaut Gordon Cooper addressing UN panel discussion on UFOs and ETs, 1985," *UFO Universe*, vol. 1, no. 3, November 1988, at www.ufoevidence.org/documents/ doc961.htm.

HYNEK, J. Allen, "Dr. J. Allen Hynek Speaking at the United Nations," November 27th, 1978, at www.ufoevidence.org/documents/ doc757.htm.

McDONALD, James E., "Dr. James McDonald's Letter and Statement to the United Nations, June 7th, 1967," at www.ufoevidence.org/ documents/doc1056.htm.

HUNEEUS, Antonio, "Statement to the Second Symposium on Extraterrestrial Intelligence and the Human Future, UN Society for Enlightenment and Transformation (SEAT)," reprinted in SEAT newsletter, December 1993.

BERLINER, Don, and STREIBER, Whitley (compiler), "International Agreements and Resolutions – United Nations," *UFO Briefing Document: The Best Available Evidence*, New York, NY, Dell, 2000.

SCHUESSLER, John F., UFOs, THE UN, AND GA 33/426," *HUFON REPORT Newsletter*, December 1992, at www.ufoevidence.org/ documents/doc748.htm.

ASSOCIATED PRESS, United Nations Hears Case for UFOs [Article about Eric Gairy, Prime Minister of Grenada], October 15th, 1978.

UNITED NATIONS TREATY ON PRINCIPLES GOVERNING THE ACTIVITIES OF STATES IN THE EXPLORATION AND USE OF OUTER SPACE, INCLUDING THE MOON AND OTHER CELESTIAL BODIES, London, Moscow, and Washington, January 27th, 1967, at www.oosa.unvienna.org/SpaceLaw/ outerspt.html.

PROPOSED UN SPACE PRESERVATION TREATY, at www.peaceinspace.com/sp_treaty.shtml.

Endnotes

Chapter 2

[1] JUNG, Carl G., "Dr. Carl Jung on Unidentified Flying Objects," *Flying Saucer Review*, vol. 1, no. 2, 1955; see also JUNG, Carl G., HULL, R.F.C. (translator), *Flying Saucers: A Modern Myth of Things Seen in the Skies*, 1958, republished Princeton, NJ, Princeton University Press, 1979.

[2] DEARDORFF, James, HAISCH, Bernard, MACCABEE, Bruce, and PUTHOFF, Hal E., "Inflation-Theory Implications for Extraterrestrial Visitation," *Journal of the British Interplanetary Society*, vol. 58, 2005, pp. 43-50.

Chapter 3

[3] ANONYMOUS, "The Lucifer Rebellion," *The Urantia Book*, Chicago, IL, The Urantia Foundation, 1955, p. 601.

[4] BROWN, Courtney, *Cosmic Explorers*, New York, NY, Dutton, 1999, p. 243.

[5] BROWN, Courtney, *Cosmic Voyage*, New York, NY, Dutton, 1996, p.158.

Chapter 11

[6] BROWN, *Cosmic Voyage*, p. 263.

Chapter 17

[7] DEARDORFF, James, *et al.*, *op. cit.*

Chapter 20

[8] See *www.echelonwatch.org*.

[9] BOURDAIS, Gildas, *COMETA: The French Report on UFOs and Defense: a Summary*, Chicago, IL, Center for UFO Studies (CUFOS), 1999.

[10]CAMERON, Grant, "UFO Studies Done and Proposed by the Carter Administration," *www.presidentialufo.com*, 2005.

Chapter 21

[11] BROWN, *Cosmic Explorers*, p. 9.

[12]PUTHOFF, Hal E., "CIA-initiated Remote Viewing at Stanford Research Institute," Austin, Institute for Advanced Studies, 1995; see also, LORA, Doris and TARG, Russell, "How I was a Psychic Spy for the CIA and found God," Institute for Noetic Sciences (IONS), November 2003.

[13] BROWN, *Cosmic Voyage,* p. 63.

[14] Scientists have discovered that Mars once had saltwater oceans. See "Mars rover sits on ancient beach," BBC News, March 23rd, 2004, at *news.bbc.co.uk/1/ hi/sci/tech/3560867.stm*. Scientists have also discovered that microbial life once existed on Mars, as evidenced by a meteor from Mars that impacted Earth. See NASA, "Meteorite Yields Evidence of Primitive Life on Early Mars," August 7th, 1996, at *www2.jpl.nasa.gov/snc/nasa1.html*. See also "Rare Mars meteorite discovered in Middle East," CNN News, May 25th, 2000, at *archives.cnn.com/ 2000/TECH/space/05/25/mars.meteorite*. Both methane and ammonia have been discovered in the current atmosphere of Mars. See WHITEHOUSE, David, "Methane on Mars could signal life," BBC News, March 29th, 2004, at *news.bbc.co.uk/2/hi/science/nature/ 3577551.stm* and WHITEHOUSE, David, "Ammonia on Mars could mean life," BBC News, July 15th, 2004, at *news.bbc.co.uk/1/hi/sci/tech/3896335.stm*. These gases can only result from living organisms or from recent volcanic activity. No active volcanoes have been found on Mars. Scientists say that life there is likely. See, e.g., DAVID, Leonard, "Life on Mars Likely, Scientist Claims," *www.space.com*, August 3rd, 2004, at *www.space.com/scienceastronomy/mars_ microorganisms_ 040803.html*.

[15] BROWN, *Cosmic Voyage*, p. 92.

[16] See "Finding and Processing Cosmic Information – Ongoing Problems of Exopolitics," at *www.exopolitics.com*, 2005.

Chapter 22

[17]CAMERON, Grant, "President Jimmy Carter's Actual UFO Sighting Report," at *www.presidentialufo.com*, 2005.

[18] President Carter's statement was later confirmed by White House special assistant media liaison Jim Purks, in a letter dated April 20th, 1979.

[19] CAMERON, Grant, "Jimmy Carter, the Nobel Prize, and Extraterrestrials," at *www.presidentialufo.com*, 2005.

[20] CAMERON, Grant, "President Jimmy Carter, 39th President, January 21, 1977 to January 20, 1981," at *www.presidentialufo.com*, 2005; see also Jimmy Carter, *en.wikipedia.org/wiki/Jimmy_Carter*.

[21] DISCLOSURE PROJECT, "Carter White House Denied UFO Info," 2003; see also DISCLOSURE PROJECT, "Disclosure, Military and Government Witnesses Reveal the Greatest Secrets in Modern History," The Disclosure Project, Crozet, VA, 2001, p. 441.

[22] JENNEY, Kay, "UFO convention speaker says we must become 'galactic citizens'," *The Mohave Daily News*, February 8th, 2003, at *www.centerchange.org/passport/030208mdn.html*.

[23] MANNION, Michael, *Project Mindshift: The Re-education of the American Public Concerning Extraterrestrial Life*, New York, NY, M. Evans and Company, 1998.

[24] THE ROPER POLL, *UFOs and Extraterrestrial Life: Americans' Beliefs and Personal Experiences*, prepared for the SCI-FI Channel, September 2002.

Chapter 23

[25] CANADIAN BROADCASTING CORPORATION, CBC archives, July 2nd, 1967.

[26] BARRETT, Peter, "The basis for the claim that 'we are facing the end of civilisation as we know it ... by the end of the century'," Wellington, NZ, Antarctic Research Center, Victoria University, 2004.

[27] BROWN, *Cosmic Voyage*, p. 173.

[28] Private communication with the author.

[29] KAPLAN, Stephen, *The Launching of the New Energy Movement*, New Energy Movement, 2004, at *exopolitics.blogs.com/exopolitics/2004/05/the_launching_o.html*.

[30] BARRETT, Peter, *op. cit.*

[31] WORLD METEOROLOGICAL ORGANIZATION, INTER-GOVERNMENTAL PANEL ON CLIMATE CHANGE (IPCC), *IPCC Third Assessment Report – Climate Change 2001*, Cambridge, UK, Cambridge University Press, 2001.

[32] SCHWARTZ, Peter, and RANDALL, Doug, "An Abrupt Climate Change Scenario and its Implications for United States National Security," Emeryville, CA, Global Business Network, October 2003.

[33] BARRETT, Peter, in a radio interview with the author, Coop Radio, CFRO 102.7 FM, Vancouver, BC, December 20th, 2004, at *www.coopradio.org*.

[34] BROWN, *Cosmic Explorers*, p. 216.